EARLY
NATIVE
AMERICANS

IN

WEST VIRGINIA

EARLY
NATIVE
AMERICANS

IN

WEST VIRGINIA

THE FORT ANCIENT CULTURE

DARLA SPENCER

THE
History
PRESS

Published by The History Press
Charleston, SC
www.historypress.net

Front cover: Artwork created by artist Susan Walton with SA Walton Studio in Florida. *Courtesy of the Ohio History Connection.*

First published 2016

ISBN 9781540200815

Library of Congress Control Number: 2016941430

Notice: The information in this book is true and complete to the best of our knowledge. It is offered without guarantee on the part of the author or The History Press. The author and The History Press disclaim all liability in connection with the use of this book.

Midway through researching and writing this book, I lost my best friend, my beloved husband, Bob. He was always there to help, whether it was washing pottery, carrying my bags and books or listening patiently while I talked for hours about archaeology. He was my rock. This book is for him.

CONTENTS

FOREWORD

During my ten-plus years of teaching Native American studies at West Virginia University, countless students have shared artifacts given to them by grandparents whose families have farmed, hunted and fished throughout this region for generations. The typical scenario involves the student opening a brown paper lunch bag or cardboard matchbox, uncovering a small item or two wrapped in cotton or paper towels and revealing some relic discovered after a new garden was tilled or a driveway was flooded out. Regardless of provenience, these earnest students *always* want to know about the early people who made these items, "How old do you think this is? How was it used? What tribes have lived in West Virginia?" In addition, not a year goes by without random inquiries from members of the general public asking about the geographical extent of the mound builder cultures, where to get a stone axe head appraised, who to call if a farmer or logger is concerned about intruding on a village site and so on.

I am not an archaeologist—my training lies in the social sciences. So my usual response to these queries is to stress the essential role of *context* in looking at any archaeological artifact, awareness of laws addressing the disturbance of human burials and theft of funerary objects and other sacred items and consideration of our collective responsibilities regarding preservation and conservation. The next step is to contact my faculty colleague and go-to expert Darla Spencer, the author of this admirable volume. She is knowledgeable, resourceful, generous and well connected to fellow archaeologists, and she has demonstrated such in numerous collaborations within the region's professional and academic communities.

Spencer's diligent research and documentation provide an invaluable resource for anyone—fellow scientist, college student or casual reader—wishing to access the archaeological evidence that helps describe West Virginia's Fort Ancient people. In addition to being well versed in the subject area, Spencer is able to articulate complex matter with her trademark fluid, objective writing style. Her characteristic attention to detail and ability to weave a multidimensional chronology make *Early Native Americans in West Virginia: The Fort Ancient Culture* a pleasure to read and ponder. Spencer's efforts allow us to traverse an archaeological landscape that previous scholarly writers, through inattention, have by default deemed an anthropological "no-man's land."

I invite you to thoughtfully approach the following pages, savoring the description, detail and nuances of Spencer's efforts in completing this work. The Fort Ancient ancestors who lived in these beautiful hills and valleys deserve the acknowledgement that Darla Spencer helps cultivate, her words nudging us along the time continuum chapter by chapter and deeply enriching our understanding that this was, indeed, home to many thousands of early people whose presence must be affirmed in any informed telling of our continent's human past.

BONNIE M. BROWN

PREFACE

A little over twenty years ago, I decided to revisit my first love, archaeology. It was a hectic time, to say the least—working and taking care of the family during the day and going to school at night—but it was one of the best decisions of my life. Since then, I have spent many hours researching the early history of West Virginia and particularly the late prehistoric/protohistoric periods and the Fort Ancient culture. Unlike other states, West Virginia archaeology has been somewhat overlooked. This book is meant to be a reference for archaeologists as well as an introduction for interested amateurs. The glossary in the back of the book will help familiarize nonarchaeologists with commonly used archaeological terms.

We know that native people occupied West Virginia for more than ten thousand years, but not much has been written about them except in archaeological journals. It is my hope that this volume will help fill that void and encourage other archaeologists to share what we know about a poorly understood part of our state's history.

ACKNOWLEDGEMENTS

Q uite a few individuals and organizations contributed to the completion of this work. I would like to acknowledge and thank the following:

The History Press and Candice Lawrence for guiding me through the preparation of the book;

Bonnie Brown of the Native American Studies Program at West Virginia University for preparing the foreword for the book;

The Smithsonian Institution and David Rosenthal for permission to use photographs from the museum's artifact collections from West Virginia;

The Grave Creek Mound Archaeological Complex and Heather Cline for permission to photograph artifacts from the facility's collections;

The West Virginia Geological and Economic Survey for permission to use material from its publications;

The West Virginia Archeological Society for permission to use material from its publications;

The Huntington Museum of Art for permission to photograph artifacts from the Adams Collection from the Clover site;

The Blennerhassett Museum and Ray Swick for permission to photograph the museum's artifact collections;

The U.S. Army Corps of Engineers, Huntington District and Aaron Smith for permission to use material from the Burning Spring Branch site report;

Cultural Resource Analysts Inc. and Mike Anslinger for permission to use material from the Burning Spring Branch site report;

MACTEC and Pat Garrow for permission to use material from the Dickinson Farm site report;

GAI Consultants and Ben Resnick and Marina Davis for permission to use material from the Logan village site report;

William Youse for allowing me to photograph the artifact collection of his grandfather Hillis Youse; and

The West Virginia Humanities Council for funding my research and other archaeological research over the years.

A special thank-you goes to Jim Kompanek of Cultural Resource Analysts for preparing the site location map.

Many thanks go to the following individuals (some now deceased) who contributed photographs used in the book: Dr. Robert Maslowski, Dr. Jeffrey Graybill, Stanley Baker, Roland Barnett, Ron Moxley, Craig Ferrell, David Martin, Harvey Allen, Bill Williams, Pat Garrow and Pamela Casto.

Special acknowledgement goes to my colleagues Mike Anslinger, Stevan Pullins, Dr. Nicholas Freidin, Dr. Robert Maslowski, Pat Garrow and Marina Davis for help reviewing portions of the text.

And finally, I would like to thank my family, who put up with my absence for much of the last year.

Chapter 1

BACKGROUND

L ong before the first Europeans entered the Ohio Valley, the hills and valleys of what is now West Virginia were occupied by native people. Since the first Europeans arrived in West Virginia in the 1700s, historians, ethnologists and archaeologists have struggled to identify the native people who once lived here. For many years, West Virginia was thought to be an "Indian hunting ground" with no long-term occupations by early native people. However, we now know that native people hunted and inhabited West Virginia for at least ten thousand years before the arrival of Europeans. Along the major rivers, farmers cannot plow their fields without exposing stone tools and other evidence of the native people who once lived here.

Native American history in North America has been described as a continuum of culture change that began with the earliest hunter-gatherer groups who entered North America and hunted the large ice age mammals during the Late Pleistocene epoch to the village-dwelling farming communities that were encountered after European contact.[1] During each consecutive period, populations grew as the native people gradually became more sedentary and developed new, more efficient ways to exploit the changing environment and its resources.

To make this continuum more manageable, archaeologists have designated time periods to organize the last fifteen thousand years or so in time. These are based on the traditions of the people who lived during each period and the changes in technology that came about as seen through the material culture, or the artifacts, that were left behind. For archaeologists, usually this is all that remains to learn about the people who lived during a specific time. For older sites, the only things that survive are stone tools.

Although general dates are given for the transitions from one period to the next, these transitions varied from region to region and are by no means firm. Usually changes in technology began near the end of the preceding period and were firmly established by the time the following archaeologically derived period began. The first clay pottery, for example, appeared at different times in different places, so the dates attributed to these changes in technology are approximate.

THE PALEO-INDIAN PERIOD

The currently accepted timeline of early North American history begins around fifteen thousand years ago at the end of the last glacial event with the arrival of the first Native American groups into North America from Asia.[2] The first known people in North America, known as Paleo-Indians by archaeologists, were a hunting-gathering people who were thought to have followed the large ice age mammals, or megafauna, across the Bering Strait into North America near the end of the geologic Pleistocene epoch. At the end of the Pleistocene epoch and the beginning of the Holocene epoch, which we are in now, the climate warmed and the glaciers retreated. Many of the megafauna were unable to adapt to the changing climate and became extinct. The native people in North America were forced to change their lifeways to survive. Smaller mammals became important food sources, and new tools were developed to hunt them. These changes in technology and lifestyle brought us into what archaeologists call the Archaic period.

ARCHAIC PERIOD (8000 BC TO 1000 BC)

At the beginning of the Archaic period, native people in North America continued to live in highly mobile, kin-based groups. They still led a hunter-gatherer lifestyle as before, traveling from area to area to hunt and collect food. The stone projectile points (spear points) developed at this time were used over a wide area, indicating that they traveled far distances. Because they traveled such distances, they were able to exploit the best chert quarries for tools, such as projectile points. The lack of evidence for nonutilitarian items also indicates a rather simple, mobile lifestyle. Near the end of the Archaic period, which lasted roughly seven thousand years, the native people became more sedentary, settled in one place and began to domesticate the first wild plants for food. These changes in lifestyle led to what archaeologists call the Woodland period.

THE WOODLAND PERIOD (1000 BC TO AD 1000)

Archaeologists traditionally distinguish the Woodland period from the preceding Archaic period by the appearance of clay pottery, the construction of burial mounds and other earthworks and the beginnings of plant domestication. However, we now know that some of these developments occurred earlier and originated at different times in different parts of the country. The first clay pottery in eastern North America was made in the Southeast around 2500 BC,[3] although it wasn't until around 1000 BC that clay pottery construction began in the Ohio Valley. During the Woodland period, the mound-building Adena and Hopewell cultural traditions flourished in the Ohio Valley.

THE LATE PREHISTORIC AND PROTOHISTORIC PERIODS (CIRCA AD 1000/1050 TO AD 1650/1700)

Around AD 1000, the lifestyles of Native Americans throughout eastern North America changed once again and became more sedentary. Throughout the Ohio Valley, the native people lived a rather similar lifestyle, occupying larger villages near rivers and streams. They began to use crushed mussel shell to temper their pottery. They used the newly introduced bow and arrow for hunting and became farmers, growing corn, beans and squash (known as the Three Sisters), as well as sunflower and other plants. These became what archaeologists call the Late Prehistoric and Protohistoric periods. During this time, the Fort Ancient people flourished in the Ohio Valley.

The Late Prehistoric period, as designated by archaeologists, is pre-European contact, and the Protohistoric (or Contact) period, refers to archaeological sites occupied after European contact in the Southeast, where European trade items, such as European metal (copper or brass) and glass trade beads, are found. In the Ohio Valley, including West Virginia, contact is thought of as beginning around 1540, when Hernando De Soto arrived in the southeastern area of North America. Soon after, European trade items began making their way inland along established trade routes between inland native groups and those living in coastal areas. At this time, European populations were living near the coast and had not yet visited inland areas like West Virginia or the Ohio Valley. Usually in West Virginia, European trade items are not found until the late 1500s to 1600s.

EARLY EXCAVATIONS IN WEST VIRGINIA

Until 1960, when the West Virginia Geological and Economic Survey (WVGS) hired Dr. Edward McMichael as the West Virginia state archaeologist, archaeological excavations at sites in West Virginia were primarily conducted by amateur or avocational archaeologists, many of whom were members of the West Virginia Archeological Society (WVAS). Several of these individuals published their findings in the *West Virginia Archeologist*, the journal of the WVAS. Many times, that is the only existing information about the site, and some sites were damaged by the excavations. While some individuals recorded details and kept meticulous notes, other excavations were lacking in documentation and sometimes rather haphazard.

LAWS AFFECTING HUMAN REMAINS

With the passage of the National Historic Preservation Act in 1966 and NAGPRA and the West Virginia state burial law in the 1990s, human remains were given some protection against indiscriminate disturbance and looting.

National Historic Preservation Act of 1966 (NHPA) and Section 106

Section 106 of the National Historic Preservation Act of 1966 requires that federal agencies evaluate the effect of all federally funded or permitted projects on historic properties, including historic buildings and archaeological sites. It also requires consultation with federally recognized Indian tribes that may have had a prehistoric presence in the area when prehistoric human remains might be affected by the project.

Native American Graves Protection & Repatriation Act (NAGPRA)

In 1990, the Native American Graves Protection & Repatriation Act or NAGPRA was enacted into law by George H.W. Bush. NAGPRA gave federally recognized Indian tribes the ability to claim human remains and associated artifacts found on federal or tribal land for reburial if the tribe could prove a direct lineal descent or cultural affiliation with the remains in question. This also applies to archaeological projects with federal funding where human remains are found.

Because there were no known Native Americans living in Fort Ancient territory in West Virginia when the first Europeans arrived, it has not yet been possible to establish the identities of most of the native peoples who once lived here or who their descendants might be. Therefore, Native American remains that have been found in West Virginia have been considered *culturally unidentifiable* under NAGPRA. Culturally unidentifiable refers to human remains and associated funerary objects in museum or federal agency collections for which no lineal descendant or culturally affiliated Indian tribe or Native Hawaiian organization has been determined.

Until the passage of the West Virginia burial law in 1991, there were no state laws addressing the excavation of human remains in West Virginia unless the project had federal funding. WV Code §29-1-8a, Protection of Human Skeletal Remains, Grave Artifacts and Grave Markers Permits for Excavation and Removal, offers some penalties for the indiscriminate removal of human remains unless conducted by professional individuals who have applied for and received a permit from the West Virginia State Historic Preservation Office. Removal of human remains without this permit is considered a felony.

TRINOMIALS

The three-part number and letter designations for recorded archaeological sites are called trinomials. The trinomial designation system was developed by the Smithsonian Institution in the 1930s and 1940s. The first number represents the state in which the site is located. West Virginia is represented by the number 46. The second part represents the county. The third part is the number of the recorded site in chronological sequence. For example, 46PU31 represents the Buffalo site, the thirty-first site recorded in Putnam County, West Virginia. When a site is registered with the West Virginia State Historic Preservation Office, its unique trinomial designation is recorded.

Chapter 2

THE FORT ANCIENT CULTURE

Fort Ancient is the name given to Late Prehistoric and Protohistoric native settlements in the Ohio Valley from southern West Virginia to Indiana between about AD 1000 and AD 1650 to 1700. The end date is largely unknown, and estimates vary from researcher to researcher. However, by the time Europeans entered Fort Ancient territory in West Virginia, the once thriving area was abandoned.

Most Fort Ancient settlements were located along rivers or streams in the floodplain. Fort Ancient villages were usually circular or oval with a number of square or rectangular post-built houses encircling an open, central plaza area and surrounded by one or more wooden post palisades. The Fort Ancient tradition includes three major traits: (1) increased reliance on agriculture, (2) increased sedentism and (3) a rise in sociopolitical complexity. However, these elements also apply to other contemporaneous indigenous groups.[4]

HISTORY OF FORT ANCIENT

The area of the Ohio Valley that archaeologists call Fort Ancient territory was explored in the 1800s by the Bureau of American Ethnology (BAE) of the Smithsonian Institution. At that time, the prevailing thinking was that the mound-building cultures that left the most visible remains in the

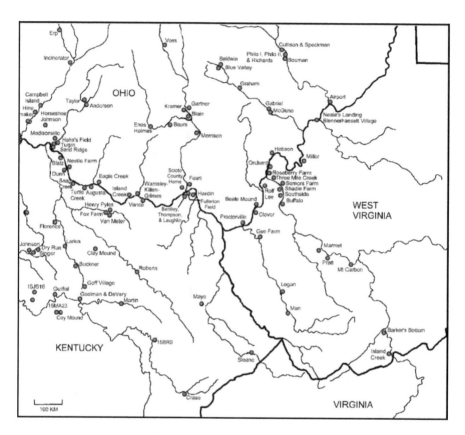

A map showing the area of Fort Ancient occupation in West Virginia and surrounding states. *Author's files, Hoffman 1997.*

form of the mounds and earthworks were not made by the ancestors of the Native Americans in North America but by a mysterious superior race. The mound explorations of the BAE during the 1880s put that idea to rest and determined that North America's indigenous people had, in fact, constructed the many mounds and magnificent earthworks that dotted the Ohio Valley.[5]

During the mound explorations, the investigators also noted and excavated nonmound sites that contained a variety of artifacts, some of European origin. William C. Mills, who excavated several of the important mounds in Ohio, first defined and named the Hopewell and Fort Ancient cultures.[6] At the time, he mistakenly believed that the Fort Ancient culture was earlier than that of the Hopewell because, to him, the Hopewell appeared the more advanced and, therefore, later culture. The Fort Ancient name was taken from the Fort Ancient earthwork site in Ohio that we now know is a Hopewell site.

In 1943, James B. Griffin defined the "Fort Ancient aspect," based on similarities in artifacts from various Late Prehistoric sites, mostly in Ohio. Village sites from southeastern Indiana to western West Virginia were included in the Fort Ancient cultural tradition by Griffin, although he designated sites in West Virginia as "related to Fort Ancient" due to similarities in pottery.[7] Today, however, most archaeologists include Late Prehistoric and Protohistoric village sites in southern West Virginia in the Fort Ancient culture.

FORT ANCIENT TERRITORY IN WEST VIRGINIA

In West Virginia, Fort Ancient territory begins on the Upper Ohio Valley south of Sistersville in the Northern Panhandle and encompasses the drainages of the Little Kanawha, Kanawha/New and Guyandotte Rivers. West Virginia contains the easternmost limits of what is known as Fort Ancient.

The northern and eastern portions of West Virginia were occupied by two other Native American groups at this time: the Monongahela people,

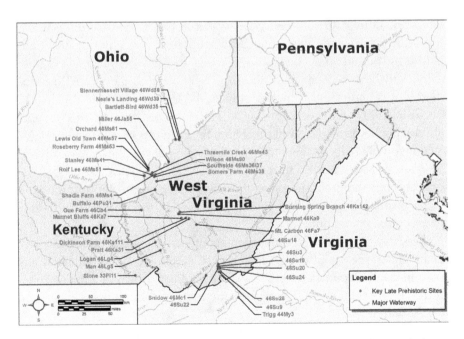

A map of Late Prehistoric and Protohistoric sites in West Virginia. *Cultural Resource Analysts Inc.; U.S. Army Corps of Engineers, Huntington District; and Jim Kompanek.*

who lived in the Northern Panhandle of West Virginia and adjoining parts of Ohio and Pennsylvania, and the Susquehannock people, who occupied parts of the Eastern Panhandle of West Virginia and adjoining parts of Pennsylvania. This volume will explore what is known about the Fort Ancient people of West Virginia.

Known Fort Ancient sites in West Virginia have been dug and collected by avocational (amateur) archaeologists for many years, and few have been systematically investigated by professional archaeologists since their discovery. For this reason, what is known about some of the Fort Ancient sites discussed in this volume is incomplete at best. Much of the information and many of the photographs included in this volume came from private collections. The sites I have chosen to discuss here are those with sufficient information to provide a good overview of Fort Ancient culture in West Virginia.

FORT ANCIENT SUBSISTENCE

Subsistence refers to the methods or actions of a particular group of people to survive. For Fort Ancient people, the primary methods of subsistence were agriculture and hunting. Native people had begun to domesticate wild plants during the preceding Woodland period, but during the Late Prehistoric period, they began to practice maize agriculture. Corn, or maize, had been recently introduced into the Ohio Valley from Mexico, where it was domesticated from a grass called *teosinte*. The Late Prehistoric Fort Ancient people began to farm, growing corn, beans, squash and sunflower. They probably used the Three Sisters method of farming, a type of companion planting where the corn formed a pole for the beans to climb, the beans provided needed nitrogen to the soil and the leaves of the squash plant covered the ground around the base of the corn, preventing weeds from growing. This method of planting was used by many American Indian cultures into historic times.

The arrival of maize had a great impact on native populations. Maize has been found at several Late Woodland period sites in West Virginia, although it was in small amounts and may have not yet been grown as a major crop. However, around AD 1000, corn became a major food source throughout Fort Ancient territory.

Corn lacks protein and other nutrients. Populations grew, but many people were malnourished. Late Prehistoric people were shorter than their ancestors and had lowered immunities. The sugar content in corn caused tooth decay, and there were many health problems caused by vitamin deficiencies. Life expectancy was shorter than before, as well. Many people died before the age of fifty and about half before thirty. Many children died before the age of six.

In addition to cultivated plants, Fort Ancient people gathered wild nuts, including hickory nuts, walnuts, acorns, hazel nuts and butternuts. They also harvested wild fruits, such as plums, papaws, sumac, wild grapes, cherries, hawthorn and hackberries.

Fort Ancient people supplemented their diets by hunting with the newly introduced bow and arrow. From faunal (animal) remains found at village sites, we know they hunted and consumed white-tailed deer, elk, black bear, raccoon, opossum, fisher, groundhog, squirrel, beaver, wild turkey and other animal species. Fort Ancient people also fished with bone fishhooks and gathered mussels from the nearby rivers and streams. Dog skeletons are common at many Fort Ancient sites; they may have used them for protection and hunting and occasionally (perhaps when hunting was poor) for food. Although native people farther west hunted buffalo, or bison, no buffalo remains have been found at Fort Ancient villages in West Virginia. It appears that buffalo did not appear east of the Ohio River until the 1700s.

FORT ANCIENT MATERIAL CULTURE

Lithic Materials

Lithic refers to tools and ornaments made from stone. The most common type of stone material used by Fort Ancient people was chert, or flint. Because of the way it breaks with a conchoidal fracture, chert can be worked to a very fine cutting edge. This characteristic makes chert perfect for cutting tools and projectile points.

During the Paleo-Indian and Archaic periods, when people traveled long distances, they were able to obtain the finest, most beautiful cherts during their travels. Multicolored Flint Ridge chert from Ohio, for example, is found in the form of projectile points throughout eastern North America.

However, during the Late Prehistoric period, when people were more sedentary and settled into villages, they used mostly locally available sources of chert. Kanawha Black Flint, or Kanawha chert, comes from central West

Virginia and is the most common type of chert found at Fort Ancient sites. In addition to being sourced from outcroppings, Kanawha chert is often found in rivers and streams as cobbles. Tools made from chert include projectile points (spear points, arrowheads), knives, hoes, discoidals and scrapers.

Another type of stone commonly used for tools at this time is locally occurring sandstone. Sandstone tools that have been found include hammerstones, axes and discoidals.

Pottery

Clay pottery vessels were first developed in the Southeast between 4,500 and 2,500 years ago in the form of shallow bowls.[8] Clay pottery making spread until its arrival in the Ohio Valley around 1000 BC, during the Early Woodland period. Before clay vessels were constructed, bowls were sometimes made from sandstone.

The first clay pottery vessels were rather crude: thick-walled and tempered with crushed stone. By the Late Prehistoric period, however, pottery vessels had become more refined and tempered with crushed mussel shells. There was a variety of surface treatments used on the outside of the vessels that were decorative and also kept the vessel from slipping when wet. Cordmarking, for example, was made by striking the vessel with a cord-wrapped paddle while still wet before firing. Later surface treatments included net or knotted net and corncob impressing.

The predominant vessel form for Fort Ancient pottery is a coil-built jar with a flared rim. Appendages like lug or strap handles were sometimes added to the rims and necks of the vessels for easier handling and suspending over a fire. Bowls and saltpans also occur.

Other decorative treatments sometimes added to Fort Ancient pottery include punctates (circular indentations) and incising around the neck. At Fort Ancient sites elsewhere, a common decoration was a guilloche with incised intertwined lines around the vessel neck.

Marine Shell Gorgets

One of the unique artifacts found at Fort Ancient sites throughout the Ohio Valley is the engraved marine shell gorget. Marine shell gorgets originated in the Southeast in Mississippian societies and began to show up at Fort Ancient villages during the Late Prehistoric period. Engraved shell gorgets can be traced to their regions of origin, indicating prehistoric trade networks in place throughout the eastern United States. Many originated in eastern Tennessee.[9]

Marine shell gorgets have been found mainly in a burial context. In eastern Tennessee, rattlesnake gorgets were found primarily with adult women and children, probably of high rank. In contrast, the mask gorget was primarily associated with men and children. The distribution of the gorgets during the Protohistoric period was thought by researchers Brain and Phillips to reflect the dispersal of people from the Southeast after European contact.[10]

Engraved marine shell gorgets were found throughout the Southeast from the Late Prehistoric period into historic times. They have been found in at least fifteen states and Canada.[11] These ornaments began to show up at Fort Ancient villages in West Virginia after AD 1450.[12]

Marine shell gorgets were cut from large marine whelks, of the species *Busycon*, found only along the Gulf and Atlantic coasts of North America.[13] Marine shell gorgets come engraved with various designs. In West Virginia, only two styles of engraved shell gorgets have been found in any number.

The first type of gorget frequently found in West Virginia is the rattlesnake gorget. The circular rattlesnake gorget is always engraved on the concave side of the shell. The basic design is a coiled rattlesnake with the body wrapped around the head. The eye of the snake is always in the center of the design and is represented by a pit circled by a series of concentric rings. The body of the snake is divided into three or four segments, represented by crosshatched, engraved lines (indicating scales), and separated by bars and concentric circles. At the end of the body, the rattle is clear in all variations. The amount of wear on rattlesnake gorgets is considerable, suggesting constant use as opposed to only ceremonial or burial wear.[14]

In West Virginia, at least ten rattlesnake gorgets have been found, although only one from the Buffalo site has good provenience. Other rattlesnake gorgets have been found at Clover, Pratt, Orchard, Marmet and Rolf Lee.

The second type of marine shell gorget commonly found in West Virginia is the mask gorget. Mask gorgets are made in the form of a human face and do not show as much wear as other styles, suggesting less frequent use.[15] The mask gorget has a distribution similar to that of the rattlesnake gorget, although it is much more widespread. Mask gorgets have been found in burials as far north as Manitoba and as far west as Montana and the Dakotas. The largest concentrations occur in eastern Tennessee, northeastern Arkansas, the western tributaries of the Mississippi River and Fort Ancient territory.[16]

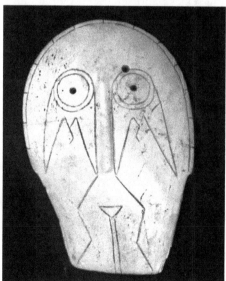

Above: A Citico-style rattlesnake gorget from the Rolf Lee village. *Harvey Allen.*

Left: An engraved Buffalo-style marine shell mask with Weeping Eye from the Buffalo site. *Grave Creek Mound Archaeological Complex, West Virginia Division of Culture and History.*

Mask gorgets are the largest of the marine shell gorgets and are made from the outer whorl of the whelk shell. The gorget is carved in the shape of a human head, and the mask design is always engraved on the convex side of the shell. On some mask gorgets, parallel zigzag lines run from the eyes down the face. These markings, called the "Weeping Eye" or "Forked Eye," have been interpreted as tears, tattooing or face painting. They have also been interpreted as the natural markings of birds of prey, such as the falcon, whose swiftness and aggressiveness were admired by native warriors. The appearance of a mask gorget in a historic Kansa war bundle seems to confirm this interpretation. Before battle, warriors opened their bundles and hung the gorgets around their necks.[17] Researchers Marvin and Julie Smith suggested that perhaps the mask gorgets were symbolic trophy heads.[18]

In West Virginia, twenty-two documented mask gorgets have been found. Of those, only eight have good provenience. Of the eight, one was found in the burial of a women, one over the face of a child and six, or 75 percent, with adult men. The predominance of mask gorgets found in burials with adult men in West Virginia is similar to the patterns found in the Southeast and elsewhere.[19]

The third type of marine shell gorget commonly found in West Virginia is the shell maskette. These are small mask gorgets that are fewer than six centimeters wide. Some maskettes are plain, and others are engraved with the Weeping Eye design. According to Penelope Drooker, the maskettes appears to be more concentrated in Fort Ancient territory than other areas, which suggests they may have originated there.[20] There have also been maskettes found that were made from larger marine shell gorgets that originated in the Southeast. Drooker also observed that the maskettes appear to have been made primarily for children.[21]

In West Virginia, at least seventeen small shell maskettes have been found, although most were found out of context. Of the eight maskettes found with good provenience, one was found with an adult man and seven with children.[22]

Unengraved shell gorgets are also plentiful throughout the Southeast and in Fort Ancient territory. According to Brain and Phillips, this is a style that was purposely left unengraved and was made throughout the span of time when other styles were being produced but appears to be more prevalent during Protohistoric and historic times.[23]

In West Virginia, plain gorgets have been found at Buffalo, Bluestone, Marmet, Orchard, Rolf Lee, Three Mile Creek and Southside. At least fifteen plain gorgets have been found in West Virginia, although only eleven

Small engraved marine shell maskettes from the Orchard site. *Harvey Allen.*

have good provenience. Of these eleven, two were found with adult men, five with women and four with children.[24]

Marine shell ornaments found in Fort Ancient territory in West Virginia that originated in the Southeast are also evidence of a major trade route between the two regions. There is evidence of a long and continuous interaction between Fort Ancient villages in West Virginia and Mississippian groups in the Southeast. There was a trade network for shells throughout eastern North America as early as the late Archaic period and an extensive exchange of finished shell items by the mid-thirteenth century.[25]

Discoidals

Small round discs made from clay or stone are common at many Fort Ancient villages throughout the Ohio Valley. These are called discoidals, or discoids. Their use in Fort Ancient society is uncertain, although they most closely resemble similar, but usually larger, discoidals that are used in a game called Chunkey, or Chunkee. It is thought that this game was played

Stone discoidals from Burning Spring Branch site. *Cultural Resource Analysts Inc. and U.S. Army Corps of Engineers, Huntington District.*

by many Native American peoples for hundreds of years. In *The Southeastern Indians*, Charles Hudson describes the Chunkey game as follows:

> *In the early colonial period, the most popular game among the Southeastern Indians seems not to have been the ball game, but the game called Chunkey. Always played by males, this was a variety of the hoop and pole game that was played by Indians throughout North America. Chunkey was distinctive in that instead of a hoop made of wood, the Southeastern Indians used a wheel-shaped disc made of carefully polished stone.*[26]

As with Chunkey stones, stone and clay discoidals are found in a variety of forms. Some are convex, some have central holes and some are incised.

Clay discoidals were sometimes made from broken pottery vessels, and some have cordmarking on one side.

Smoking Pipes

Another item commonly found at Fort Ancient villages is the smoking pipe. Used throughout prehistory and among historic American Indian peoples, smoking was both a religious and personal event. The earliest pipes found in West Virginia were in Adena mounds and may have had a ceremonial function. During the later Fort Ancient period, smoking pipes were found with many burials, predominantly those for men. In addition to ceremonial uses, these pipes appear to have been personal items that were used by men throughout life and accompanied them in death.

Unlike many objects that appeared to follow a distinct pattern in form, smoking pipes came in a variety of shapes and materials. These include clay and many types of stone, such as quartz, steatite, limestone and sandstone. Pipe shapes are often in the form of animals; others have been found in platform, ovoid, elbow or keel shapes.

Smoking pipes from the Orchard site illustrating a variety of shapes and materials found on Fort Ancient smoking pipes in West Virginia. *Roland Barnett.*

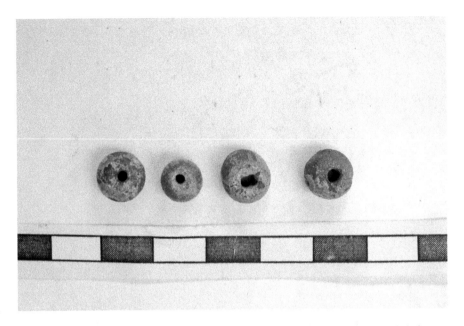

European blue glass trade beads from the Rolf Lee site. *Grave Creek Mound Archaeological Complex, West Virginia Division of Culture and History.*

European Trade Items

European trade items that began to show up at Fort Ancient sites in the Ohio Valley during the sixteenth century were of two types: glass trade beads and metal artifacts (copper or brass). These items are thought to have come from the Southeast and were traded inland along established trade routes from native peoples in contact with Europeans.

Chapter 3

FORT ANCIENT CHRONOLOGY

EARLY FORT ANCIENT
(CIRCA AD 1000/1050 TO 1250)

The Early Fort Ancient period in West Virginia was named the Roseberry phase by researcher Dr. Jeffrey Graybill for the Roseberry Farm site in Mason County, which is an Early Fort Ancient village with pit houses and a burial mound.[27] The sites included in the Roseberry phase are distinctly different from earlier Woodland period occupations. Graybill suggested that the development was with in-place Woodland peoples possibly through interactions with Mississippian groups to the south.[28]

During the Early Fort Ancient period, pottery consisted of shell-tempered constricted-neck jars with plain surfaces and diametrically opposed angular strap handles, semilunar lugs and other handles. Castellations were common, and decoration was usually a band of punctates (circular indentations) or linear gashes around the neck of the vessel.[29]

Projectile points during this period were triangular arrow points with convex, straight and concave bases. Ground and chipped stone celts, biconcave and sometimes perforated discoidals and semiplatform and short-stemmed elbow pipes are also present. Other items that were made during this period are diamond-shaped cannel coal pendants, abrading stones, hammerstones, nutting stones and flake knives.[30]

Bone, antler and shell items include deer antler projectile points, flakers and drifts. Turkey metatarsal and deer ulna awls, as well as splinter bone awls, are found. Turkey bone beads, needles, beamers, hairpins and pendants are common, as well as turtle shell cups, perforated mussel shell hoes, marine shell pendants, whelk columnella shell beads and shell disc beads.[31]

Houses during the Early Fort Ancient period included pit houses and surface structures. The floors of pit houses were dug below the ground surface. Other features include hearths, pits and burials. Burials were predominantly flexed and in basin-shaped pits. At Roseberry Farm, the only known Fort Ancient village with a burial mound, more than twenty-five burials were encountered within the excavated portion of the mound, leading investigators to estimate that possibly two to three hundred interments are there.[32]

Ten Roseberry phase sites have been documented in West Virginia. They are usually located on high terraces along larger streams. Most are known primarily through surface surveys. All of the documented sites are habitation sites with a range of artifacts. In addition, all are village sites more than 0.3 hectares in size. Only three Roseberry phase sites have been systematically excavated so far: Roseberry Farm (46MS53) in Mason County, Miller (46JA55) in Jackson County and Bartlett Bird (46WD35) in Wood County.[33]

By the Early Fort Ancient period, the Fort Ancient people in West Virginia had acquired corn and were practicing maize agriculture. Maize remains have been found in at least two Roseberry phase sites: Roseberry Farm and Bartlett Bird. In addition to maize, other cultigens were found at sites from this period, as well as a variety of nuts, seeds and plant remains. Animal remains from this period included a variety of species, with white-tailed deer being most common.[34]

MIDDLE FORT ANCIENT (AD 1250 TO 1450)

The Middle Fort Ancient period was designated Blennerhassett phase by Graybill for the Blennerhassett Village site in Wood County.[35] Eight village sites from this period have been documented in West Virginia, although only one, the Blennerhassett village (46WD38), has been thoroughly investigated.[36] Other sites from this period include Lewis Old Town in Mason County (46MS57) and Chiyoda in Wood County (46WD52).[37]

LATE FORT ANCIENT (AD 1450 TO ABOUT 1700)

After about AD 1450, there appeared to be increased interaction among Fort Ancient villages throughout the Ohio Valley. This was especially evident in the similarities in pottery found on Fort Ancient sites from this period. Fort Ancient archaeologists called this period the Madisonville Horizon for the Madisonville village in Ohio.[38]

New artifact types also appeared during this period. Madisonville-style pottery appears, and engraved marine shell gorgets, Marginella and Olivella marine shell beads, vasiform smoking pipes, clay figurines, claw-shaped cannel coal pendants, bone beads, bipointed knives and bifacial endscrapers are found. Eventually, European trade items began to appear on village sites during this period.[39]

Village sites were larger, located in the floodplain and heavily fortified with palisade walls, perhaps for protection. No pit houses have been found from this period, and the surface structures are larger. Individuals were interred in simple pits and sometimes were buried within house floors or in the midden.[40]

Sometime between 1640 and 1730, Fort Ancient territory in West Virginia and much of the Ohio Valley was abandoned.[41] Pressures from Iroquois Nations over the fur trade and the introduction of European diseases have been mentioned as possible factors, but the why and when remain largely unknown.

Chapter 4

FORT ANCIENT SITES IN WEST VIRGINIA

THE BUFFALO SITE (46PU31)

The Buffalo site is located on a high first terrace on the east bank of the Kanawha River in Putnam County south of the town of Buffalo. The site is multicomponent and was occupied once in the Late Archaic period, once in the Woodland period and twice during the Late Prehistoric and Protohistoric Fort Ancient periods. The Archaic component was reported by Bettye Broyles in 1976.[42] The Fort Ancient villages were well known by locals and were collected for many years.

The earliest known Fort Ancient occupation at Buffalo has a radiocarbon date of AD 1170/1275, and the later occupation has a date of AD 1680/1651.[43] The two Fort Ancient occupations consisted of two slightly overlapping villages, with the later village also called the Downstream village.

Between 1963 and 1965, archaeological excavations were undertaken by then state archaeologist Dr. Edward McMichael from the West Virginia Geological and Economic Survey (WVGS).[44] At the time, McMichael thought that the villages might be destroyed by development. The Buffalo village excavations were one of the first systematic archaeological investigations conducted in West Virginia. Most of the excavations were of the Downstream village, about 15 percent of which was excavated.

Across the site at 150- to 200-foot intervals, 20-foot-wide trenches were excavated.[45] The excavations revealed the two overlapping villages, both oval in plan view (from above), with post molds of several rows of rectangular

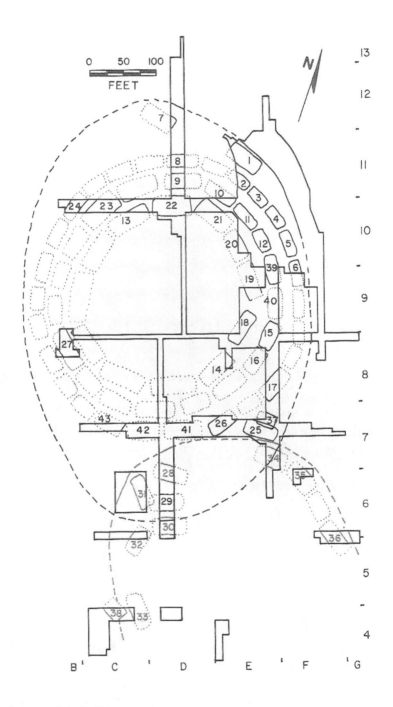

A site plan map of the Buffalo excavations showing the two overlapping villages and the areas excavated. *West Virginia Geologic and Economic Survey, Hanson 1975.*

houses with rounded corners surrounding a central, open plaza area. Both villages were surrounded by several rows of palisade lines, indicating repair over time.[46]

Excavations also uncovered numerous fire basins, fire hearths, earth ovens, refuse pits and storage pits from the Downstream village. Fire basins and hearths were primarily within houses. Four storage pits were also found within the houses. Refuse disposal was predominantly along the palisade lines.[47]

The houses at the Buffalo village were relatively large, rectangular structures with rounded corners. The average house size was twenty feet wide by thirty feet long with two center posts. Wall posts were spaced approximately eighteen inches apart.[48]

A total of 562 human burials was reported from the Buffalo village excavations, all but one from the Downstream village. Four hundred and four (71.5 percent) of the individuals were buried in the floors of houses, usually along the walls. The rest were interred throughout the village. All but one of the interments were within simple pits. One individual was interred in a stone box grave. Burial positions consisted of 53.7 percent fully extended, 9.8 percent flexed from the waist down and 23.5 percent fully flexed; 84 percent of the interments were placed with their heads pointing between north-northeast and south.[49]

The age and sex determinations of the burial population at the Buffalo site were compiled by James Metress and consisted of 61.5 percent adults, 6.7 percent young adults, 6.7 percent child and 12.0 percent infant; 41.0 percent were male and 59.0 percent female.[50]

Thirteen individuals appeared to have died violent deaths, indicated by embedded projectile points (arrowheads) and suggesting possibly warfare. The embedded points were found with men, women and children, and the arrow points were made from nonlocal cherts, possibly indicating nonlocal raiding parties.[51]

Twenty-three percent of the individuals at the Buffalo village were buried with grave goods, consisting of tools, containers and ornaments. Many of these items were made from European copper and brass traded down the line from Native American groups in contact with Europeans. Eleven individuals were interred with copper or brass artifacts that were usually sheet metal tubes that may have been used as hair ornaments. Of these individuals, nine were adults, one was a child and one was unidentifiable. Six individuals were female, two were male and three were unidentified.[52]

Twenty-six other individuals were buried with one or more marine shell gorgets or pendants around their necks. These included marine shell

Marine shell ornaments from the Buffalo site. *Grave Creek Mound Archaeological Complex, West Virginia Division of Culture and History.*

gorgets and beads that were traded into West Virginia from Native American peoples who lived in the Southeast. Both of these groups of items were probably considered status goods because of their scarcity, and therefore, individuals buried with these objects may have had some standing in the community. Of these individuals, eleven were adults, two were young girls, eight were children, three were infants and two were unidentified. Of the adults, four were male, six were female and the remaining individual was unidentified.[53]

Fifty-one other individuals were interred with marine shell beads and small pendants. Of these, twenty-seven were adults, two were young adults, eleven were children, five were infants and six were unidentified. Of the adults in this group, eleven were male, thirteen were female and three were unidentified. One child was interred with a white glass seed bead of European origin.[54]

In addition to those individuals interred with trade items, 29.7 percent of burials contained some type of container. These included pottery vessels and turtle shell cups. Three individuals were interred with bead bone "skirts." One was an adult male, and one was an adult female.[55]

Subsistence

The villagers at Buffalo grew maize and squash and possibly beans in gardens around the village. One probable charred bean was recovered.

Maize, supplemented by meat from hunting, probably made up a major part of the diet. Both eight-row and ten-row maize varieties were found at the site.[56]

Faunal Remains

A total of 1,699 animal remains, originating from seventy-eight species, was recovered from the Buffalo village. Most of these probably added to the diet of the village residents.[57] As with most Fort Ancient villages, the white-tailed deer was the most common mammal found at the Buffalo site, with 746 individuals found, or 44 percent of the total faunal assemblage from the site. In contrast, the remains of only 2 elk were recovered. The next most common mammal species found at the village was gray squirrel, followed by raccoon, black bear, beaver, woodchuck, opossum, rice rat, gray fox, bobcat, cottontail rabbit, elk, fox squirrel, gray wolf, skunk, mountain lion, chipmunk, otter, muskrat, fisher, long-tailed weasel and mink. The remains of 25 domestic dogs were recovered. These were small animals and probably weighed no more than fifteen pounds. Butchering marks indicated that they were occasionally eaten.[58]

There were thirty species of birds from the site, the most common of which was the wild turkey. Other common bird species found were ducks, crows, sandhill cranes, Canada goose, snow goose, turkey vulture, several varieties of hawks, bobwhite, passenger pigeons, Carolina parakeet, raven, several varieties of owl, woodpecker and grouse.[59]

Ten species of reptiles were recovered and included several varieties of turtles and snakes. Two amphibians, both bullfrogs, were recovered. Thirteen species of fish were also recovered.[60]

Lithic Materials

Lithic materials from the Downstream village consisted of triangular chert bifaces (arrow points), granite and chert axes (celts), chert choppers, chert knives, chert gravers, sandstone saws, drills, scrapers, hammerstones, sandstone whetstones, a single sandstone mano, chert and granite picks, stone pestles and anvils.[61]

Bone Tools

Bone tools from the Buffalo site included fishhooks, beaver incisor chisels, antler handles, antler flaking tools, antler projectile points, bone splinter awls, deer ulna awls, deer metacarpal awls, turkey tarso-metatarsal awls and bone beamers.[62]

Additional Tools

Fourteen mussel shell hoes were recovered from the Buffalo village. They were made from halves of freshwater mollusks and hafted by drilling a hole in the shell and inserting a long stick and were probably used for gardening.[63]

Ornaments

MARINE SHELL GORGETS

At least thirteen marine shell gorgets were recovered from the Buffalo site. Two large mask gorgets have been found, though one is in such a poor state of preservation that it is impossible to tell if it was engraved. The other mask gorget recovered was the archetype for the Buffalo-style mask gorget as designated by Brain and Phillips, who conducted an extensive analysis of Mississippian marine shell gorget styles.[64] It is still one of the most well-preserved, artistic examples of the style.[65] Five small marine shell maskettes were also found at the Buffalo village, two engraved and three unengraved.[66]

The only known example of a Brakebill-style rattlesnake gorget found in West Virginia was found at the Buffalo site with the burial of a child.[67] Found with the rattlesnake gorget were six irregular-shaped shell pieces, each with two holes. Two of these pieces show engravings indicating that they were cut from a rattlesnake gorget.[68]

Five plain round shell gorgets were also found at Buffalo, one decorated with four holes. In addition, there are numerous smaller shell pendants, beads, discs and at least one inner portion (columnella) of a whelk shell from the site, which could indicate that some of these ornaments were manufactured locally from imported marine shell.[69]

SHELL BEADS

There were five types of shell beads found at the Buffalo site. Disc shell beads were thin perforated discs cut from freshwater or marine shell. They were then ground and drilled through the center. Around 1,200 disc beads were found in seventeen burials. They were found in lots of 10 or 20 and appeared to be sewn on clothing. Other disc beads were strung onto necklaces and bracelets.[70]

Barrel-shaped shell beads were made from whelk shell columnella, the center of the shell, that were ground and drilled. These were found in fifteen burials in quantities from one to one hundred. Tubular beads were also made from whelk columnella and were longer than they were thick. These were found in seven burials in quantities from one to eighteen. Hemspherical shell beads were found in one burial and appeared to be used like buttons at the end of a string to keep the string from slipping through holes of gorgets.[71]

Marginella shell beads are unmodified small marine shells that were strung as beads. They were found in seven burials in quantities from one to forty-eight.[72]

ANIMAL BONE BEADS

Animal bone beads were also used as ornaments, and some were sewn onto clothing. Barrel-shaped bone beads were made from deer long bones cut into sections, ground and polished. These were found in eight burials. Their locations suggest they were strung five or six together and hung on the hems of garments. Tubular bone beads were also found, although not with burials, suggesting they had a use other than decoration. These were primarily made from bird bone shafts and were ground and polished. They may have represented a type of gaming piece.[73]

BONE TINKLERS

Bone "tinklers" were made from deer phalanges (foot bones) that were hollowed out. A hole would be drilled through one end for suspension. They were probably sewn onto garments in a similar way as brass cone tinklers were used during the historic period.[74]

PENDANTS

Numerous animal teeth were drilled and used as pendants. These included teeth from elk, bears, dogs and other small mammals. The elk and bear teeth were found with burials.[75]

Mussel shell pendants in the shape of a claw were found with four burials. Three cannel coal claw-shaped pendants were also found in the village midden. Another pendant made from the whelk shell columnella was also found. In addition, two stone pendants were recovered. The smaller of the two was roughly made, and the lower edge was serrated. The larger pendant was decorated with parallel incised lines.[76]

HAIR ORNAMENTS

Assorted hair ornaments were found from various materials at the Buffalo village. Six long animal bone pins were found that were thought to be hairpins. One example was grooved for decoration. Copper and brass tubes were also found behind the heads of some of the remains that appeared to be attached to the individual's hair. The tubes ranged from forty-three to sixty-eight millimeters in length and were found with three burials.[77]

Two bone hair combs were also found with burials. These consisted of two flat sections of bone with "teeth" notched in one end.[78]

EAR ORNAMENTS

An item commonly found at Fort Ancient villages is the marine shell ear ornament. This consists of a set of two discs with "stems." The stem was thought to be inserted through the ear lobe and a cord was used to string through a hole in the end of each stem to tie at the back of the head or neck. Ear ornaments were found with three burials at the Buffalo village.[79]

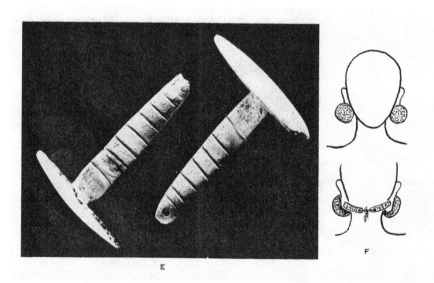

A photograph and diagram of marine shell ear ornaments from the Buffalo site. *West Virginia Geological and Economic Survey, Hanson 1975.*

Leisure Artifacts

Leisure artifacts are items that are neither utilitarian nor decorative in function but appear to be used for relaxation and amusement. It appears that, although the residents of the Buffalo village spent much of their time gardening, hunting and maintaining village structures for survival, there was also time for leisure activities, such as games and music.[80]

Musical Instruments
Twelve bird bone whistles were found at the Buffalo village. Eleven had four drilled holes, and one had three. Two of the most complete specimens were 6.3 and 11.3 centimeters long. The best-preserved example still produced a shrill high-pitched whistle when recovered from the site. Two notched rib bone musical rasps were also found at the site.[81]

Gaming Pieces
Bones that were thought to have been used for games were found made from sections of deer antler and bone that were ground and polished. In addition, round discoidals made from pottery, hematite, cannel coal and sandstone were found that may have also been used in leisure games.[82]

Smoking Pipes

Five smoking pipes were found at the Buffalo village. Two were vasiform pipes, two were bird effigies (one with a human head in its talons) and one was a disc platform pipe made from red Ohio pipestone. Two ceramic pipe stems were also recovered from the site.[83]

Clay Figures

A number of small clay effigy figures were also found at the Buffalo village. These may have been made for the children by village potters with bits of leftover clay. One of the figures in the form of a human arm has markings that resemble tattooing.[84]

Small clay figures from the Buffalo site. The small clay "arm" in the lower left appears to have tattoo markings. *Ron Moxley.*

Pottery

During their analyses of pottery from the Buffalo site, both Lee Hanson and Jeffrey Graybill noted the occurrence of corncob- and net-impressed surfaces.[85] However, subsequent analyses of the same pottery failed to recognize corncob-impressed surface treatments, possibly because this surface treatment typically occurs over another treatment and looks very similar to fabric impressions.

Hanson described the pottery from the Buffalo site as "nearly all common shell-tempered Fort Ancient types," although he noted two exceptions: "two roughened varieties, one done with a corncob and the other with knotted cordage, which must be considered rare and not meriting a formal description."[86] Hanson also noted that the corncob roughened was confined to the rims of cordmarked vessels and the knotted cordage roughened (knotted net) "is similar, but with finer impressions to New River Knot Roughened and Net Impressed" as defined by Evans.[87]

In a recent study, a total of 2,096 shell-tempered pottery sherds from the Buffalo site was examined from the collections at the Grave Creek Mound

Above: A rim portion of Fort Ancient Madisonville-style pottery vessel from the Buffalo site. *Grave Creek Mound Archaeological Complex, West Virginia Division of Culture and History.*

Right: Pottery sherds from the Buffalo site with impressions of corncobs with kernels intact. *Grave Creek Mound Archaeological Complex, West Virginia Division of Culture and History.*

Archaeological Complex in Moundsville. Most of these were collected during McMichael's excavations at the Buffalo village in the early 1960s. The most common surface treatment was cordmarking (1,134 sherds, or 54 percent), followed by plain and smoothed (676 sherds, or 32 percent). Next in frequency were corncob impressed (126 sherds, or 6 percent), corncob with cordmarking (76 sherds, or 4 percent), simple stamped (36 sherds, or 2 percent), burnished (21 sherds, or 1 percent) and knotted-net impressed (14 sherds), incised (9 sherds), corncob and knotted-net impressed (1 sherd) and simple stamped and cordmarked (1 sherd) all at less than 1 percent.[88]

It appears that the Fort Ancient–period pottery assemblage from the Buffalo village included a combination of Madisonville-style vessels and vessels with corncob impressing and other surface treatments that are not typically found at Fort Ancient villages in the Ohio Valley but are commonly found in Virginia at sites occupied by Siouan-speaking people.[89]

In 1971, the Buffalo village was added to the National Register of Historic Places.

BURNING SPRING BRANCH (46KAI42)

The Burning Spring Branch site was first identified and recorded in 1979 by Tom Kuhn working for the Huntington District U.S. Army Corps of Engineers. At the time, Kuhn identified fifty-nine nondiagnostic chert artifacts and an unknown quantity of thermally altered rock probably collected from the eroded bank of the river. He interpreted the site as a seasonal camp of unknown age.[90]

The Burning Spring Branch site was located in an undeveloped parcel of level Kanawha River terrace on the north side of the confluence of Burning Spring Branch and Kanawha River, about ten miles south of Charleston. Boundaries of the site were formed by Burning Spring Branch to the south, disturbed industrial land to the north, the Kanawha River to the west and a lack of archaeological deposits to the east. The site was primarily forested with a cleared area of about 0.6 hectares (1.5 acres) used for a vegetable garden.[91]

Between 1995 and 2002, Cultural Resource Analysts Inc. (CRA) conducted archaeological excavations at the site in advance of constructions for the Marmet Lock Replacement project. The work was completed under contract with the Huntington District U.S. Corps of Engineers to achieve compliance with Sections 106 and 110 of the National Historic Preservation

Act. The primary goal was to determine if the site was eligible for the National Register of Historic Places and, if eligible, to mitigate any adverse effects to the site that might result from the lock replacement project.[92]

The investigations enabled the Huntington District to determine that the site was eligible for the National Register of Historic Places and to mitigate adverse effects to the site through Phase III data recovery excavations. The excavations also resulted in the identification of Native American occupations dating to the Archaic, Woodland and Late Prehistoric Fort Ancient periods, as well as historic industrial and residential remains associated with the occupation of the Reynolds family during much of the nineteenth century and a small historic cemetery thought to predate the Reynolds occupation of the site.[93]

After evidence for a Fort Ancient village was uncovered, the surrounding palisade line was traced northward into the woods by hand excavations revealing the outer palisade of the village extending as an arc to the riverbank northwest of the garden. With the size of the village defined, the decision was made to remove the plow zone from the entire area of the village. Once the newly stripped surface of the village was exposed, additional evidence of the Fort Ancient occupation was revealed, including the documentation of additional houses and features, as well as human burials.[94]

An aerial view of Burning Spring Branch village showing palisade line and house patterns. *Cultural Resource Analysts Inc. and the U.S. Army Corps of Engineers, Huntington District.*

The exposed semicircular Fort Ancient village was highly organized, with twenty-four rectangular post structures situated around an open central plaza that lacked evidence of a central post. Except for one structure that was attached to the outermost palisade, structures at the site were enclosed by at least one palisade. An exterior wall of several of the houses included small, circular post structures interpreted as possible storage facilities.[95]

The Precontact Fort Ancient village was built on a bluff above the Kanawha River. In addition to the post molds from the palisades and houses, there were 153 Late Prehistoric features found. These included sixty-four pits, forty basins, twenty-five burials, fourteen shallow midden remnants and five rock clusters. Features were distributed within structures, between structures, within the central plaza and around the periphery of the village. Burials were found in the open central plaza, within structures and around the edge of the village. Preservation at the village was relatively poor.[96]

With the plow zone removed, 133 test units were excavated into the Late Prehistoric village midden. A total of 57,424 artifacts was recovered, with the categories and type of materials consistent with those reported for other Late Prehistoric sites in the area. Artifacts made of chert and ceramics were most common.[97]

The preponderance of evidence indicates that unlike many other Fort Ancient villages, Burning Spring Branch was occupied for a relatively short time. Evidence like the lack of a thick village-wide midden, the relatively small number of features (including human burials) and the relatively small artifact assemblage recovered—as well as the lack of burned structures, minimal evidence of rebuilding and repair of structures and palisade walls and lack of superimposed structures—suggests a relatively short duration of occupation.[98] The village was radiocarbon dated at circa AD 1400–1500. No European trade items were found at Burning Spring Branch, offering further proof that the site was occupied before European contact.[99]

Human Remains

The remains of twenty-five individuals were interred at Burning Spring Branch associated with the Fort Ancient occupation of the village. Once discovered, the documentation, recovery and treatment of the remains and associated materials followed protocols set forth in a plan of action developed by the Huntington Corps of Engineers through consultation with federally recognized Indian tribes.[100]

Lithic Materials

Lithic materials from the Late Prehistoric Fort Ancient component at Burning Spring Branch were recovered from test units, features and structures. A total of 46,314 lithic flakes, 2,885 pieces of thermal shatter, 162 cores, 4 core tools, 75 retouched flakes, 443 bifacial implements, 3 unifaces, 8 ground stone implements and 55 cobble tools was recovered.[101]

The bifacial artifacts included 165 triangular arrow points, all of which appear to be associated with the Fort Ancient component. In form and size, these points are consistent with those recovered from other Late Prehistoric sites in the region and are typically typed as Madison, Hamilton or Fort Ancient. These are different from Late Woodland Levanna points, a few of which were also recovered from the site. Of the Late Prehistoric points recovered, 148 were manufactured from locally available Kanawha chert.[102]

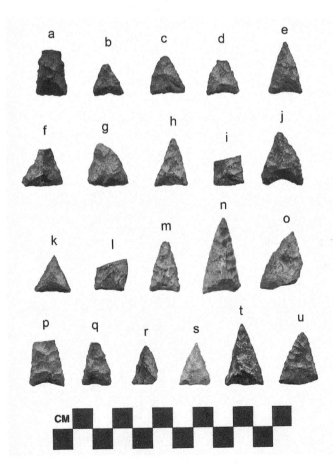

Triangular arrow points from the Burning Spring Branch Fort Ancient component. *Cultural Resource Analysts Inc. and the U.S. Army Corps of Engineers, Huntington District.*

Discoidals

There were twenty-four whole or partial stone discoidals recovered from the Fort Ancient component at Burning Spring Branch. All were manufactured from locally available materials. Twenty-three were made from sandstone, and one was from a highly polished indeterminate stone. Twenty-two of the discoidals were manufactured by grinding and pecking, two were ground with a central indentation and one was polished with an indentation. One of the ground and pecked discoidals exhibits an X on one surface.[103]

Forty-two ceramic discoidals or fragments were recovered from the Late Prehistoric feature, test unit and general surface contexts at Burning Spring Branch. All were created from shell-tempered ceramic vessel fragments. The surface treatments on some were from the original pottery vessels. Twelve of the discoidals had center holes. Surface treatments that were identifiable included three cordmarked, one corncob impressed and one indeterminate textile treatment.[104]

Smoking Pipes

Two stone pipe fragments were recovered from the Fort Ancient component at Burning Spring Branch. One, manufactured from pipestone, was

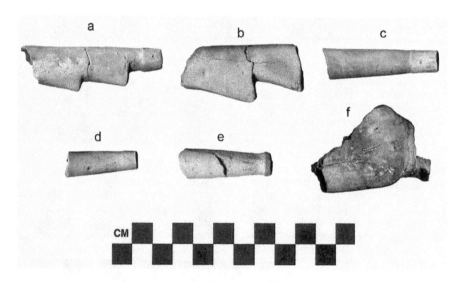

Clay pipe stems from the Burning Spring Branch, some with zigzag stem design. *Cultural Resource Analysts Inc. and the U.S. Army Corps of Engineers, Huntington District.*

recovered inside Structure 1. It was an oblong-shaped bowl fragment measuring approximately 28.4 by 23.4 millimeters. Another pipe fragment was recovered from a test unit near the outermost palisade wall. Due to the condition of the fragment, the diameter could not be estimated.[105]

Thirty-six ceramic pipe fragments were recovered from the Fort Ancient component at Burning Spring Branch. These consisted of sixteen bowl fragments, sixteen stem fragments and four indeterminate pieces. They were recovered from throughout the village, including the structures and central plaza.[106] Two clay pipe stems with a zigzag shape, similar to one from Man in Logan County, were recovered.

Faunal Materials

Faunal materials were recovered from cultural features, test units and the general surface during the course of the Phase III investigation. A total of 53,913 animal remains was recovered from all components at the site. Of these, 44.5 percent were identified to class, genus and species level. Twenty-two mammals, twelve birds, at least one amphibian, nine fish and fifteen reptiles were identified. There were also three snail species recovered and an undetermined number of mussel species.[107]

The Fort Ancient component at Burning Spring Branch produced amphibian, avian, mammal, fish, reptile, vertebrates and invertebrate remains. A dog was the only domesticated animal in the assemblage. Wild resources that probably contributed to the diet at the village included large, medium and small birds: wild turkey, wild goose, ruffed grouse, duck and passenger pigeon. Mammals likely to be food included white-tailed deer, raccoons, squirrels, beavers, rabbits and bears. There were also fish, river mussels and turtles in the remains recovered. Deer and large mammals contributed the largest amount of meat, followed by birds, including wild turkey, and eastern box turtle. Mammals that probably didn't contribute to the diet included bobcat, possible coyote, gray fox, skunk, opossum, ground squirrel, chipmunk and rats and mice.[108]

Paleoethnobotanical Remains

The most common plant remains found in the Fort Ancient component at Burning Spring Branch were wood charcoal. Species of wood included hickory (the most frequent), walnut, pine and oaks, ash and black locust. Other plant remains included carbonized nutshell, carbonized corn and carbonized seeds, including beans and bean fragments, and carbonized nutmeat. Seeds included grass, bean, sumac, grape, chenopodium, sumpweed, bedstraw, blackberry/raspberry/dewberry, false Solomon's seal, rush, sunflower, blueberry, dogwood, oat, papaw, persimmon, viburnum and wheat. The wheat and oat remains are thought to have been a historic intrusion at the site.[109]

A total of 3,587 corn fragments including corncobs and fragments, corn cupule fragments, corn cupules, corn kernels, corn kernel fragments, and corn stalk fragments were recovered as evidence that the inhabitants of the village practiced maize agriculture. Seven pepo (squash) fragments were also recovered from the site.[110]

Pottery

A total of 83,837 ceramic vessel sherds was recovered from the Burning Spring Branch village, 46,461 (57 percent) of which were shell tempered. Only ceramic fragments from nonburial contexts were analyzed. Identifiable exterior surface treatments on shell-tempered ceramics included cordmarked (38.0 percent), fabric (net) impressed (17.0 percent), burnished (6.6 percent), plain (6.5 percent) and corncob impressed (6.0 percent). Approximately 73.9 percent of the cordmarked ceramic sherds had Z-twist cordage twist direction.[111]

Much of the pottery recovered at Burning Spring Branch was different from typical Fort Ancient Madisonville-style pottery normally recognized in West Virginia and the Ohio Valley in that it had corncob impressions on the outer surface of the vessel. In addition, unlike typical Madisonville-style pottery vessels that have cordmarked bodies and plain or smoothed necks, much of the pottery at Burning Spring Branch exhibited impressed necks to the rim of the vessel.[112] The final analysis of the Burning Spring Branch ceramics confirmed that 37.9 percent (by weight) of shell-tempered pottery rims and necks had corncob impressing alone or with another surface treatment.[113]

In 2008, a technical report was submitted by CRA detailing the results of archaeological excavations completed at the site by the Huntington District Corps of Engineers to mitigate adverse effects on the Burning Spring Branch site. The information included in the report provides the public and scholars with information about the site and helps advance the

A shell-tempered pottery vessel rim with corncob impressing on neck. *Cultural Resource Analysts Inc. and the U.S. Army Corps of Engineers, Huntington District.*

understanding of pre-European contact habitation along the Kanawha River and in the region. The investigations at the Burning Spring Branch site on the Kanawha River documented human occupation there from about 1645 BC to AD 1500 and into the historic period. A nearby salt spring had probably attracted people to the area for thousands of years. The investigations at Burning Spring Branch provided one of the most detailed and complete records for the Late Prehistoric, Late Woodland and Late Archaic/Early Woodland Transitional periods ever documented in West Virginia.[114]

CLOVER (46CB40)

The Clover archaeological site covers around eleven acres on a second terrace overlooking the Ohio River about twelve miles upriver from

Huntington in Cabell County, West Virginia. It is located within the U.S. Army Corps of Engineers' Green Bottom Wildlife Management Area in Lesage, West Virginia. Eighteen archaeological sites, dating from Paleo-Indian to historic times, have been found within Green Bottom.[115]

Clover was also a multicomponent site, with occupations dating from the Paleo-Indian, Woodland and Late Prehistoric to Protohistoric Fort Ancient. The Late Fort Ancient Protohistoric occupation dates between AD 1473 and 1611, and archaeologist Dr. Nicholas Freidin, who conducted excavations at the site with the Marshall University Field School, proposed a date of occupation for the village of mid- to late sixteenth century.[116] Like many archaeological sites in West Virginia, the Clover site had been surface-collected for many years.

History of Excavations

In the 1880s, the Bureau of Ethnology conducted investigations on the burial mounds in the Ohio Valley, including much of West Virginia.[117] Colonel P.W. Norris, who conducted the excavations in West Virginia, collected a pottery vessel from what was described as an Indian cemetery in Cabell County and may have been the Clover site. The vessel is a typical Fort Ancient Madisonville-style pottery vessel similar to those found at Fort Ancient villages in the Ohio Valley.

James Griffin also described the Clover component in *The Fort Ancient Aspect*. He reported three raised areas at the site about two hundred feet in diameter and five feet high. These may have been mounds from the Woodland period, but years of plowing have destroyed these features.[118]

Griffin described the burial of a child about seven years old accompanied by eighty-six Marginella shell beads, six shell discs and four shell pendants. At the child's feet were an additional ninety-two Marginella beads, and near his/her pelvis was a small clay effigy of a "quadruped."[119]

Griffin also described flat, rectangular celts; triangular arrow points; ovoid knives; flint drills; and sandstone abrading tools and hammerstones found, as well as drilled bear, elk and fox teeth; awls; fishhooks; and bone beads. Copper artifacts included four pear-shaped pendants and three notched copper beads. A red pipestone pendant was also found.[120]

Several fragments of pottery vessels were recovered, and one pot was able to be restored. Griffin described the pottery as typical Fort Ancient Madisonville cordmarked. A small ceramic human head was also found.[121]

Above: A Madisonville-style pottery vessel collected by the Bureau of American Ethnology probably from the Clover site (Catalogue No. Thomas 53810). *Department of Anthropology, Smithsonian Institution.*

Right: European copper and/or brass metal artifacts from the Clover site. *Adams Collection, Huntington Museum of Art.*

In the 1970s, a local collector, John J. Adams, donated his artifact collection to the Huntington Museum of Art. The collection contained nearly four thousand artifacts from the Clover site. A fluted point was included in the Adams collection from the Paleo-Indian occupation at the site.[122]

The Clover village is considered to have been occupied late in the Late Fort Ancient sequence dating after European contact. Exotic European copper and brass fragments, copper or brass cutouts in the form of a mouse and a fish and three glass beads were also found at Clover, suggesting trade with other native groups in contact with Europeans.[123]

In addition, several marine shell gorgets and Marginella shells were found at the Clover site, indicating trade with Indian groups in the Southeast. At least one Citico-style rattlesnake gorget was found at Clover, as well as two small marine shell maskettes.[124]

Several stone smoking pipes were also found at the Clover site. At least one steatite gorget was found, as well as several stone gorget fragments.

A Citico-style marine shell rattlesnake gorget from the Clover site. *Adams Collection, Huntington Museum of Art.*

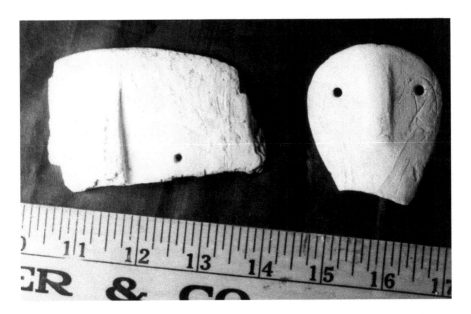

Two small marine shell maskettes from the Clover site. *Grave Creek Mound Archaeological Complex, West Virginia Division of Culture and History.*

Stone smoking pipes from the Clover site. *Adams Collection, Huntington Museum of Art.*

A steatite gorget from the Clover site. *Adams Collection, Huntington Museum of Art.*

From 1984 to 1986, the Marshall University Archaeological Field School conducted the first systematic investigations of the Clover site. The objective of the excavations "was to determine the horizontal parameters of the Fort Ancient village site and to ascertain the vertical nature of the archaeological deposits."[125] What was revealed were intact deposits dating from the Late Prehistoric to the Contact or Protohistoric periods. The occupation covered a semicircular area with a central area devoid of features, indicating a central plaza.[126]

During several seasons at the Clover village, 48.00 square meters (516.67 square feet) of the site was excavated. In 1987, a technical report was submitted to the West Virginia State Historic Preservation Office describing the results of the excavations. The Fort Ancient Clover occupation had been originally about 3.0 hectares (7.4 acres) in size, but about one-third of the site had been partially destroyed by erosion from the Ohio River. Features within the village included five burials, a fire basin, postholes and several pit structures along the western portion of the village where the excavations were conducted.[127]

The initial excavation uncovered a dark-brown midden layer about forty centimeters thick between the surface plow zone and the sterile silt loam subsoil. Although there was village debris throughout, there was a distinct thicker midden ring that surrounded the village. Post molds were uncovered within the domestic zone, but the area excavated was not sufficient to determine if they were from houses. No sign of a surrounding palisade was noted, although one might be present.[128]

The midden zone contained mussel shells, ground stone, animal bone, bone and shell tools, pottery sherds, fire-cracked rocks and charcoal. Triangular arrow points and chert debitage from locally available Kanawha chert were also found, as well as deer antler arrow points. Bone fishhooks, fish vertebrae and fish scales were found at the Clover village, suggesting the inhabitants of the site fished in addition to hunting for their food. One test pit contained burned mussel shells, and others contained faunal remains, as well as carbonized corncobs, indicating an agricultural lifestyle.[129]

Five burials were found inside the midden area and in the western sector of the village, and another burial was discovered in an eroded bank wall during floods in 1985. One burial was that of a girl about twelve years old. Around her neck was a necklace of marine Marginella shell beads and mussel shell pendants, and she wore a bracelet of shell beads around each wrist. A fragment of copper was found under her left ear. A small shell-tempered pottery vessel was placed near the child's head. Inside was an ashy substance.[130]

The second burial was that of a man about twenty-five years old. There were no items buried with this individual. The two other burials were incomplete. One was an infant about eighteen months old buried with a cannel coal-claw pendant. The other may have been a bundle burial reburied from his/her original grave. The individual is thought to be an adult woman. The fifth burial was uncovered in 1986 and was an extended adult of undetermined sex.[131]

A number of postholes and small pits were also found, indicating a possible shelter, although these were not fully excavated. A test pit contained burned materials, including mussel shells, faunal remains and carbonized corncobs, indicating maize agriculture.[132]

Pottery

Pottery was abundant at Clover. The pottery was tempered with crushed mussel shell and was coil built. Much of the pottery was typical Fort Ancient Madisonville style with cordmarked bodies and smoothed or plain necks, some with strap handles. There were also small numbers of simple stamped, knotted net and corncob-impressed pottery sherds from the Clover village.[133] Small human and animal effigies made of clay were also found, possibly made by or for the children or as appendages on pottery.[134]

Lithic Materials

Chert triangular projectile points, scrapers, drills and knives were found, as well as stone tools, stone smoking pipes and cannel coal and slate ornaments. Hammerstones, anvils, celts and whetstones made from chunks of quartzite, sandstone and chert cobbles were also recovered. Steatite smoking pipe bowls were also found at the Clover site.[135]

Bone Tools

Animal bone tools recovered from Clover included bone fishhooks, deer antler points and hollow bird-bone whistles. Bone needles, awls, beamers and deer antler flakers were also recovered. Items of personal adornment from animal bone were also found, such as bone beads and "tinklers" made from deer toe bones.[136]

Shell

Freshwater mussels from the adjacent Ohio River were no doubt eaten, and the shell was crushed for pottery temper. Mussel shell was also cut into pendants and beads for personal ornaments. Marine shell Marginella beads as well as the aforementioned marine shell gorgets were also found at the Clover village, indicating trade with native groups near the coast and in the Southeast.[137]

European Trade Items

Fragments of copper and brass and European trade beads were also found, indicating a Protohistoric date for the site in the mid- to late sixteenth century.[138]

In 1992, the Clover village was placed on the National Register of Historic Places, and the same year, it was designated a National Historic Landmark.

Dickinson Farm (46KA111)

The Dickinson Farm site is a large multicomponent prehistoric site in the town of Quincy, about fifteen miles south of Charleston, in Kanawha County, West Virginia. The site is located on the right bank of the Kanawha River on an alluvial point bar. This location no doubt provided prehistoric residents with needed resources for survival. The level point bar was high and dry year-round, and chert outcrops were located in the nearby hills. The river would have provided fish and shellfish to eat.[139]

The site was recorded in 1983 by members of the Kanawha Chapter of the West Virginia Archeological Society (WVAS), which conducted limited excavations at the site. They recovered lithic and ceramic artifacts and several features dating to the Middle Archaic, Late Archaic, Late Archaic/Early Woodland transitional, Early Woodland and Middle Woodland periods. Further investigations indicated that the site had significant cultural deposits dating from the Early Archaic to the Late Prehistoric periods.[140]

Three years later, during investigations for the nearby Chelyan Bridge Replacement project, the University of Pittsburgh documented evidence of the site again with three additional clusters of artifacts given trinomials 46KA111A, 46KA111B and 46KA111C in the area of the site.[141]

Again, during Phase I archaeological work for the Kanawha County Schools prior to construction of the new Riverside High School, a portion of the area near the site was investigated. During that investigation, surface artifacts that were recovered indicated occupations from the late Paleo-Indian to Late Prehistoric periods. Further Phase II testing of two high-density artifact clusters produced artifacts ranging in age from Early Archaic to Late Prehistoric periods from the plowzone.[142]

The following year, Cultural Resource Analysts Inc. conducted Phase I testing for a proposed pipeline near Midland Trails Elementary School. Again, at that time, artifacts were discovered in the general area of the Dickinson Farm site, including a Late Archaic biface and a cordmarked ceramic vessel sherd.[143]

In 2005, Walmart Stores Inc. contracted with MACTEC Engineers and Consulting Inc. to perform a reconnaissance survey in the area of the Dickinson Farm site to locate a suitable location for a new Walmart store. With previous knowledge of intact prehistoric sites in the local area, MACTEC conducted a Phase II survey to determine whether such deposits would be affected by the store construction. The testing included surface survey, excavation of eight one- by one-meter test units, backhoe stripping of eleven areas with possible cultural features and a geoarchaeological analysis of fifteen backhoe trenches and nine Geoprobe cores.[144]

During the surface survey, 260 lithic artifacts were collected that included hafted and unhafted chert bifaces, unifacial tools, two chipped stone hoes, a prismatic blade, a core and chert debitage. Thirty cultural features were identified, including probable earth ovens, fire pits and trash pits. The eight one- by one-meter test units all contained cultural materials, and four of them contained features. The artifacts collected included 5,248 chipped stone lithic items and a large nutting stone. Collected bifaces included a Brewerton Side Notched, two Morrow Mountain bifaces and a reworked Big Sandy biface. Fragments of two Kirk Corner–Notched points and one Adena biface were also found.[145]

The Phase II investigation demonstrated that the site was intact and that deeply buried cultural deposits extended across most or all of the study area. There was evidence of occupations dating from the Early Archaic on the terraces, a Middle Woodland occupation on the levee and a possible Late Prehistoric Fort Ancient village on the west end of the levee. MACTEC recommended an intensive Phase III data recovery be conducted on the study area to fully evaluate the property.[146]

During the Phase III data recovery, approximately 623 cubic meters of sediment was removed by hand, and approximately 4,660 cubic meters was

A partially excavated pit house showing the dark stain of the house floor and surrounding circular post molds from the house walls. *Pat Garrow.*

stripped mechanically. In three areas, the remains of domestic structures were located. One of these was an Early Fort Ancient pit house that was totally excavated.[147]

Pit houses have been found at several Early Fort Ancient village sites in West Virginia, including Roseberry Farm (46MS53) in Mason County and Blennerhassett village (46WD38) and Bartlett Bird (46WD35) in Wood County. The subterranean structures were used by Native Americans throughout the Southeast and other regions. In West Virginia, they are mainly found at Early Fort Ancient villages.

After the plow zone was mechanically stripped, a dark, amorphous stain measuring about four to six meters across was noticed in the soil. This would turn out to be the six-meter-long pit house. Cleaning of the surface revealed a dark, greasy stain and twenty-three possible post molds. Excavations revealed clusters of well-preserved burned timbers and posts a few centimeters below the top of the stain. Surrounding the burned wood was a sandy layer rich in artifacts, including many large ceramic sherds and fire-cracked rock.[148]

It appeared that the pit house was constructed over a pit that had been excavated into the subsoil. A large number of features was visible in the pit house floor, including a series of post molds mostly on the sloped edge of the pit. Many post molds were in pairs. The pit house had a level floor and steeply sloping, nearly vertical walls from thirty to sixty centimeters high.[149]

Excavations of the pit house reveal clusters of burnt timbers from house. *Pamela Casto.*

The fill of the pit house contained many artifacts associated with the Fort Ancient occupation, including small triangular bifaces, ceramic pottery vessels, cannel coal beads and discoidals, as well as other items from the Woodland and Late Archaic periods. There were no artifacts above the charred timbers, indicating the house had burned, fallen and was abandoned.[150]

Lithic Materials

A triangular hafted biface manufactured from Kanawha chert from the Dickinson Farm pit house. *Pat Garrow.*

Lithic materials from the pit house included fifty-nine unhafted bifaces, sixty-two hafted bifaces, fourteen unifaces, two cores, 14,566 pieces of lithic debitage, seventeen groundstones and six hammerstones. Triangular points were the most common of the lithic bifaces. The lithic assemblage also included some types of hafted bifaces typically associated with the Late Archaic or Woodland periods. The material of manufacture was predominantly Kanawha chert.[151]

Pottery

Ceramics recovered from the pit house included 12,083 pottery sherds, only 2,221 of which were greater than a half inch. Of this number, 2,057 were considered indeterminate and included chert, grit, grog, leached, limestone, sand, sandstone, shale, shell and siltstone tempers; 163 ceramic vessel sherds were shell tempered and considered Fort Ancient. These included shell and leached shell tempers and brushed, cordmarked, fabric-impressed, plain, eroded and indeterminate surface treatments.[152]

Faunal Materials

The pit house also contained faunal materials. Bone preservation at the site was fair to good, although some bones were not well preserved and most were fragmented. Of the 320 faunal specimens from the site, 95 percent were calcined. Five white-tailed deer remains were recovered, as well as those of other mammals and turtles. Six cows, sheep or goats were also recovered that were no doubt intrusive from later historic occupations.[153]

Paleobotanical Remains

Plant remains were also found in the pit house from the Fort Ancient occupation. These included corn cupules and kernels, suggesting maize agriculture, as well as hickory nut, black and other types of walnut, grape, sumac and persimmon.[154]

Radiocarbon Dates

Radiocarbon dates were obtained from three samples of charcoal from the pit house. The dates of AD 1280 to 1400, AD 1170 to 1330, AD 1340 to 1400 and AD 1270 to 1420 are internally consistent and indicate that the pit house was constructed sometime during the Early to Middle Fort Ancient period.[155]

GUE FARM (46CB4) AND SALT ROCK PETROGLYPHS

The Gue Farm village site is located on the floodplain of the Guyandotte River near the town of Salt Rock in Cabell County, West Virginia. The village site is on private property and has never been systematically investigated, although it has been collected by amateur archaeologists for years. While there is little information available about the Gue Farm village, part of its significance comes from its proximity to the Salt Rock petroglyphs.

A marine shell mask with the Weeping Eye design was reported from Gue Farm, as was a European glass trade bead, indicating a Protohistoric period of occupation.

Salt Rock Petroglyphs

Petroglyphs are images that are engraved or incised into stone. Archaeologists distinguish between two types of prehistoric rock art: *petroglyphs*, images pecked or carved on rock, and *pictographs*, images painted on rock. Pictographs are not commonly found in West Virginia, but many are found in the western United States.

Most petroglyphs are thought to date to the Late Prehistoric or Protohistoric periods, although there is no actual method of dating the engravings. The Salt Rock petroglyphs in Cabell County are perhaps the only datable images in West Virginia because of their possible association with the Gue Farm village nearby. The petroglyphs are carved on two large boulders about one hundred yards from the northeast bank of the Guyandotte River.

The first written observation of the Salt Rock petroglyphs was in the book *Ancient Monuments of the Mississippi Valley*, written by Squier and Davis in 1848. In this book were descriptions and drawings of the rocks. The Salt Rock petroglyphs presently include two large stones. Squier and Davis described three other rocks at the site that are no longer visible.[156]

On the top of one of the stones is a six-foot figure thought to possibly be a shaman with a Weeping Eye mask. Because of their proximity to Gue

Salt Rock petroglyphs near the protohistoric Gue Farm. *Author's collection.*

Farm, where a marine shell Weeping Eye mask was reportedly found, the engravings are also thought to date to the Protohistoric period. The side of the second stone of the Salt Rock petroglyphs is also covered with engravings, including a figure with a deer head and a fish or serpent body.

Logan (46LG4)

Under the present town of Logan, in Logan County, West Virginia, was a Native American village that appears to have been last occupied during the Fort Ancient period. Logan was formed in 1824 and named for Chief Logan, a Mingo Indian chief well known in local history. When the town was incorporated in 1852, it was named Aracoma, after the daughter of Chief Cornstalk, and in 1907, the name was changed back to Logan.[157]

The Logan village site is located on a terrace along the Guyandotte River, a tributary of the Ohio River, within the one-hundred-year floodplain. The Logan village was first recorded with the state in 1962 by Dr. Edward McMichael with the West Virginia Geological and Economic Survey (WVGS). At the time, it was described as a "prehistoric village and burial ground; skeletons frequently found in building activities."[158] The village site was thought to have been largely destroyed by the building of the town.

In 1971, the site was rerecorded by Sigfus Olafson, a founding member of the West Virginia Archeological Society (WVAS). At that time, the site was described as "a heavily occupied Late Prehistoric village and earlier occupations, all now under buildings and paved streets."[159] In a supplement to the registration form, Olafson disagreed with earlier writings from Logan County historian Henry Clay Ragland in 1896, who had described the village as a Shawnee settlement occupied as late as 1780. Olafson took issue with the late date for the settlement and, from artifacts found by residents of the town, concluded that the village was more likely a Fort Ancient occupation.[160]

In 2011, GAI archaeological consultants were hired by the West Virginia General Services Division to conduct archaeological investigations at Logan for the construction of a new state office building. The project was within the boundaries of the previously recorded Fort Ancient village. The project did not have federal participation and, therefore, did not fall under Section 106 of the National Historic Preservation Act of 1966 or the West Virginia Division of Culture and History guidelines, which meant that early consultation with federally recognized Indian tribes was not required.[161]

In January 2011, during construction, prehistoric Native American remains were inadvertently exposed. At that time, the West Virginia State medical examiner was contacted, and because of the age of the remains, the West Virginia Division of Culture and History was notified. The remains were sent to a physical anthropologist at the Smithsonian Institution, who confirmed they were the remains of two Native American individuals.[162]

With guidance from the West Virginia Division of Culture and History, an ad hoc committee was formed to develop a plan for dealing with Native American remains and conditions under which burials could be excavated and removed. Committee members included representatives from Native American tribes, the Council for West Virginia Archaeology and the West Virginia Archeological Society. Through this consultation, a burial plan was developed for the excavation and removal of any future human remains found at Logan. Following consultation, the focus of the archaeological investigations for the new office building shifted to identifying and removing burials that would be directly affected by the construction.[163]

GAI consultants' investigations identified eighty-six features within the project area. These consisted of thirty-nine burials (representing forty-one individuals), twelve refuse pits, eight thermal pits, two storage pits, two features of unknown function, two midden remains and eight post molds. In addition to the previously described features, over two hundred post molds, four historic features and nine recent noncultural features were documented. Two other burials were encountered but not included in GAI's investigations. One, consisting of several individuals, was excavated before the contract with GAI was undertaken, and the second was found in a trench and back dirt pile around a burst water pipe outside the study area. The human remains and 6,951 associated funerary items were given to the Seneca Nation for reburial.[164]

Under the agreed-on burial plan, no photographs were taken of the interred individuals or any associated burial items. Nineteen of the forty-one individuals identified were interred with personal ornaments. These individuals may have achieved some status in the community, although all five of the infants in the burial population had associated funerary objects buried with them.[165]

Burial pits were predominantly ovoid in shape. Most burials were extended and articulated, with heads oriented toward the east. Ages of the individuals at Logan were determined, where possible, based on dentition, growth plate fusion and the size or stature of the individual. There were five burials that appeared to be that of an infant, toddler or very young child. There were eight individuals who appeared to be older children or adolescents. Twenty individuals appeared to be adults or young adults. The ages for eight individuals could not be determined. Most of the infants were located near the center of the study area.[166]

Due to poor preservation and/or the absence of diagnostic skeletal elements, it was not possible to determine the sex of all the individuals in the burial population. Six individuals are thought to be male and four female. The genders of the remaining individuals are unknown.[167]

Items of personal adornment were the most common type of funerary objects found. These included Marginella shell and other marine shell necklaces, pendants and bracelets and marine shell gorgets. One adult individual was interred with a Marginella shell necklace and with a marine shell gorget and a skirt made of 127 tubular animal bone beads. Another individual, an infant, was buried with a marine shell gorget engraved with a Birdman motif on his/her torso.[168] This is the only instance of this type of gorget reported so far in West Virginia.

Bone skirts are a fairly common personal ornament found at Fort Ancient sites. Because of the time and materials used to construct one, they are

Tubular bone beads, marine shell gorget and Marginella shell beads from the Logan village. (Photograph is not from 2011 excavations.) *Craig Ferrell.*

thought to represent status items. One adult individual was found with a skirt made of 146 tubular bone beads and 260 turkey phalanges.[169]

Three other individuals had bone bead skirts as well as a container with associated funerary objects. One child and another infant/child with bone skirts also had a pottery vessel with them. Another interment, a young adult, was buried with a bone skirt and a turtle shell cup.[170]

Several adult individuals were buried with caches of projectile points and tools. One contained a ceremonial blade; Hamilton, Madison and untyped projectile points; a celt; red ochre; bone pins; and a sandstone rock. This may have been an individual who specialized in stone tool production. Another individual was buried with triangular projectile points made from Kanawha chert, a vasiform stone pipe and marine shell. The burial of another individual contained a clay pipe, a polished river agate gaming stone and five pieces of chert debitage, and yet another individual was interred with a clay smoking pipe that appeared to have a cordmarked decoration.[171]

The technical report produced by GAI Consultants in 2012 detailed the analysis of 2,994 prehistoric artifacts and 10 historic-era materials from nonburial contexts. These investigations produced information about burial practices, material culture and subsistence practices for the Late Fort Ancient occupation at the Logan village.[172]

Artifacts recovered from nonburial contexts were divided into three general material types: lithics, ceramics and faunal materials.

Lithic Materials

The lithic material assemblage included 627 stone artifacts from a nonburial context. These artifacts consisted of 9 bifaces, 1 uniface, 1 core, 352 pieces of lithic debitage, 5 cobble tools, 3 groundstones and 1 piece of red ochre. Raw material types included sandstone (41.8 percent, mostly fire-cracked rock), Kanawha and Kanawha-like chert (31.0 percent), Paoli chert (15.9 percent), chalcedony (3.2 percent), Breathitt chert (0.8 percent), Sonora-like chert (0.5 percent), Haney chert (0.2 percent) and St. Louis Green chert (0.3 percent). The remainder consisted of unsourced chert, sandstone and red ochre.[173] Projectile points recovered included three Madison triangular, one Jack's Reef Corner Notched and one Woodland triangular biface.[174]

Faunal Materials

A total of 1,664 faunal specimens, including bone and shell, was recovered from a nonburial context at Logan. The assemblage included a wide range of species, including deer, black bear, dog, squirrel, turkey, turtle and fish. As at most Fort Ancient sites, deer was the most common mammal recovered.[175]

Pottery

Ceramic analysis was conducted on 703 pottery vessel sherds recovered from nonburial contexts at the Logan village. Nearly 80 percent of the ceramic assemblage was shell-tempered. Other tempers included grit, sandstone, shell and sandstone, leached and indeterminate. Cordmarking and smoothed cordmarked were the most common surface treatments, with approximately 30 percent of the shell-tempered pottery sherds analyzed. Other surface treatments on shell-tempered pottery included corncob impressed, fabric impressed, indeterminate impressed, net impressed, indeterminate, plain, smoothed and exterior missing.[176]

Radiocarbon Dates

One radiocarbon date of AD 1770 was reported by Maslowski, Niquette and Wingfield.[177] The ceramics and European trade beads recovered from the Logan village would indicate a Protohistoric date for the Fort Ancient occupation.[178]

MAN VILLAGE (46LG5)

In June 1954, an article appeared in the *Charleston Gazette* that began as follows: "Man, June 21-(AP)-An Indian burial ground has been unearthed by construction equipment at the site of a new hospital here. Skeletons, pottery fragments, shells and assorted trinkets were unearthed Saturday during excavation at the South Man location where a United Mine Workers hospital is under construction."[179]

The Late Prehistoric Fort Ancient Man site is a located on the eastern bank of the Guyandotte River south of the town of Man in Logan County. The site also contained an earlier Woodland occupation, although most of the excavations were of the Fort Ancient occupation. The site was located near several creeks, making it a desirable location. The newspaper article was the first indication of a Late Prehistoric Native American village at Man. Within days, members of the West Virginia Archeological Society (WVAS) and others descended on the site to perform salvage excavations as the building was erected. Because of the haste of the construction, only a few artifacts were recovered. When the WVAS members arrived, the topsoil had been removed, and foundations for the hospital had been dug.[180]

Subsequent excavations by members of the WVAS uncovered a number of features, including the post molds of a palisade surrounding the village as well as fire hearths, refuse and storage pits and burials. At least thirty burials were uncovered. Many of the burials were of children. Nine burials were excavated by members of the WVAS. Some of the individuals were buried with shell and bone beads, but no metal artifacts were noted. One infant was buried with a small clay pottery vessel. Several refuse pits were discovered containing bones and teeth of bear, deer and elk, as well as fish bones, mussel shells and broken pottery sherds.[181]

In the spring of 1982, permission was given to members of the Guyandotte Chapter of the WVAS to excavate eight two- by two-square-meter units on the hospital property. Excavations uncovered fire hearths, earth ovens, trash pits, storage pits, post molds and sixteen more burials. Many of the burials contained bone beads, Marginella and Olivella marine shell beads, cannel-coal pendants and drilled animal teeth. More excavations were conducted in 1983, and in 1984, excavations were conducted on the grounds of the high school about two hundred feet south of the hospital by members of the WVAS. In 1985 an additional thirty-seven two- by two-meter units were dug to delineate the boundaries of the village.[182]

The Man village contained such features as fire hearths, earth ovens, refuse pits, storage pits and many post molds. In addition, two possible palisade lines were discovered in 1985. A central post mold was also uncovered surrounded by seven other post molds.[183]

Numerous burials were found, some with large stone slabs covering the burial. This type of burial is uncommon in West Virginia but similar to the Slone site in Pike County, Kentucky.[184] Many of the burials appeared to be persons of status and contained animal bone beads, Marginella and Olivella marine shell beads, cannel-coal pendants and drilled animal teeth. Burials were flexed, partially flexed and extended. Between 80 and 120 burials were thought to have been uncovered during the construction of the hospital. In addition, 17 burials were uncovered by the Guyandotte Chapter of the WVAS and 9 by other members.[185]

Subsistence

During the Late Prehistoric Fort Ancient period, the residents of the Man village lived a similar lifestyle to that of many other Native Americans at the time. Much of their time was spent on hunting, farming, gathering and preparing food. Many animal bones, such as from deer, bear and elk, were found at the site. Mussel shells from the nearby river also provided another food source. Nutting stones were found that were probably used in the fall for gathering and processing nuts for winter storage. Charred corncobs were also found in a storage pit, indicating that the residents of the Man site practiced maize agriculture and probably grew corn, beans and squash (the Three Sisters), as did many other native groups at the time.

Pottery

Pottery was the most common artifact found. Most was shell tempered, although some was tempered with grit and sand. Most of the surfaces were cordmarked. The rims were straight or flared, and some were decorated. Some of the pottery had strap handles.

A small reconstructed pottery bowl from Man. *Craig Ferrell.*

Shell-tempered pottery sherds with knotted net impressions from Man. *Craig Ferrell.*

Pottery vessel rim sherds with corncob impressing from Man. *Grave Creek Mound Archaeological Complex, West Virginia Division of Culture and History, Spencer 2006.*

A clay smoking pipe from the Man site with zigzag handle similar to one from Burning Spring Branch. *Craig Ferrell.*

Approximately thirteen thousand pottery sherds were recovered from the Man site, all from the hospital grounds. About 86.4 percent of the pottery collected was from the Late Prehistoric occupation, and 11.0 percent of the pottery was from the Woodland occupation. Pottery vessels found at Man were mostly shell tempered with plain, cordmarked, knotted net-impressed and corncob-impressed surfaces.[186]

Smoking Pipes

A clay smoking pipe was found at the Man village that is nearly identical to two found at Burning Spring Branch village. Both village sites date to around the same period, about AD 1400 to 1500 (pre-European contact).

Lithic Material

Lithic materials from the Man village included 138 triangular bifaces, drills, flint chipping tools, scrapers, hammerstones, whetstones, groundstone celts, abrading stones, flint knives and grinding and nutting stones. One hundred and one well-made stone discoidals were found in the midden and the features. These were made from sandstone, slate, cannel coal and pottery. Some were decorated with incised designs and some with punctates, although the majority were plain. A black stone smoking pipe was also found. Three cannel-coal beads were found in the midden, and twenty cannel-coal claw pendants were found at the site.[187]

Bone Tools

The artifact assemblage from Man also included bone awls, deer antler tine points and flakers, drilled elk teeth, canine teeth, a drilled bird claw, drilled turkey digit, drilled fish vertebrae, barrel-shaped and tubular animal bone beads, pendants, hairpins, chisels made from beaver teeth and a fragment of a bone whistle.[188] One young girl was buried with a beaded skirt that was decorated with 326 deer leg bone beads and 341 drilled turkey digit beads. Two elk antlers that were thought to be used as hoes were found in a refuse pit.[189]

Marine Shell

In addition to the many marine Marginella and Olivella shell beads and conch or whelk shell Columnella beads found with burials, an unusual marine shell gorget engraved with what appears to be a snapping turtle was also found.[190] The turtle gorget is unlike any of the marine shell gorgets found in the literature and most resembles the spider gorget with the circle and cross motif on its back. The circle and cross symbolism also indicates a connection with other Native American groups in the Southeast.

Radiocarbon Dates

Two radiocarbon dates were obtained from the Man village site. The Fort Ancient occupation dated to AD 1450, or pre-European contact, and the Woodland occupation was dated at AD 810, plus or minus fifty-five years.[191]

The radiocarbon dates for the Man site place it in the same period as Burning Spring Branch (46KA142) in Kanawha County. Both of these sites contained a greater frequency of corncob-impressed pottery than do earlier and later Fort Ancient sites in West Virginia.[192]

Marmet Bluffs (46KA7)

The Marmet Bluffs site was recognized early as a prehistoric campsite and collected by amateur archaeologists for many years. Systematic archaeological investigations were not conducted at the site, which is now largely destroyed. Marmet Bluffs was located on a knoll on a peninsula between the Kanawha River and Lens Creek upriver from the town of Marmet. The Marmet village site (46KA9) is located north of Marmet Bluffs on the other side of Lens Creek.[193]

When the West Virginia Archeological Society (WVAS) began recording archaeological sites, the site was given the name Marmet Bluffs and the trinomial 46KA7. The site was visited by Dr. Edward McMichael, Sigfus

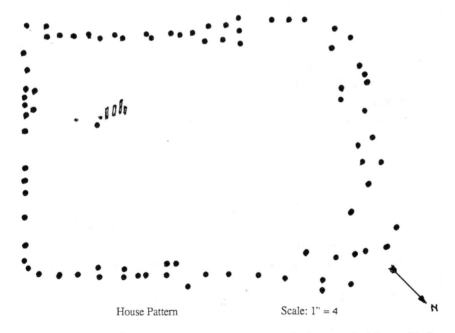

House Pattern   Scale: 1" = 4

This plan view of a post mold pattern represents a rectangular house at the Marmet Bluffs site. *From Youse, "Marmet Bluffs," West Virginia Archeologist.*

Olafson and Oscar Mairs in 1961 and was surveyed at that time by surface collecting and the excavation of a few small test pits.[194]

When the West Virginia Turnpike was constructed along the foot of the adjacent hills, excess fill material was dumped on part of the Marmet Bluffs site. In July 1972, during the grading for a new drive-in theater, part of the site was exposed. With cooperation from the bulldozer operator, Pete McDowell and Hillis Youse arranged to investigate several exposed features, including a house pattern, a fire pit and two trash pits. The rectangular house pattern investigated was located near the lower end of the site. The pattern consisted of eighty-one post molds from three to five inches in diameter forming an outline of a house about fifteen by twenty feet in area. Evidence was also found indicating the house had burned.[195]

Within the house at floor level were found two triangular bifaces (arrow points), a small diamond-shaped piece of worked slate and a side-notched biface. Within some of the post molds were sandstone fragments, chert debitage, worked chert (including a rough drill and a small projectile point preform) and a piece of rubbed hematite. Another Adena-type biface was found about a foot below ground surface made from Flint Ridge chert.[196]

About one to two hundred feet upriver from the house was a fire pit around six feet in diameter and two trash pits three to four feet in diameter and four to six feet deep containing camp debris. Included was chert debitage, worked pieces of chert, pottery vessel sherds, mussel shell and animal bone consisting of turtle shell fragments, pieces of bear and deer mandibles and a deer molar.[197]

A portion of one human skeleton was disturbed by the surface grading. The skeletal material was recovered and reburied.[198]

Pottery

An analysis of fifty-six pottery vessel sherds recovered from the site was conducted in 1983 by Robin M. King. Fifty-two of the sherds were shell tempered, and four were grit tempered. Twenty-two were cordmarked, twenty-five were plain, four were smoothed, one was knot-roughened, three were disturbed and one was net impressed. Pottery from the site indicated a primary Fort Ancient occupation of the Marmet Bluffs site with a possible earlier Woodland occupation.[199]

Radiocarbon Dates

A sample of charcoal from the house was submitted for radiocarbon dating, and the resulting date was AD 1285. The date indicates an Early to Middle Fort Ancient occupation for the Marmet Bluffs site.[200]

MARMET VILLAGE (46KA9)

The Marmet village is a Protohistoric Fort Ancient village located on the south bank of the Kanawha River in the town of Marmet in Kanawha County, West Virginia. Originally, there were two sites near this location separated by Lens Creek. However, the upper site, Marmet Bluffs (46KA7), was destroyed by construction. Like many sites in West Virginia, the Marmet village has never been professionally investigated but was collected

A Madisonville-style pottery vessel from Marmet village with cord marking on the body and a smoothed, or plain, neck (Catalogue No. A113584). *Department of Anthropology, Smithsonian Institution.*

Left: A marine shell gorget from Marmet village (Catalogue No. A113585). *Department of Anthropology, Smithsonian Institution.*

Below: A redstone serpent effigy smoking pipe from Marmet village (Catalogue No. 113784). *Department of Anthropology, Smithsonian Institution.*

by amateur archaeologists for many years. The village site is located in a residential area of Marmet, and many of the artifacts and burials found there resulted from house construction or repair by local residents.

In the 1880s, during the mound explorations of the Ohio Valley by the Bureau of American Ethnology, the Marmet village was investigated by Colonel P.W. Norris, who conducted the excavations in West Virginia. At that time, the Marmet village was called the Brownstown Works, described as "an ancient earthen enclosure encompassing 6 to 8 acres" and said to be partially used for defense by early white settlers.[201] Cyrus Thomas also reported numerous "relics" found in the streets and gardens and on the banks of the Kanawha River, including brass ornaments, stone implements and decayed human bone, although none of these was witnessed by him personally.[202] Colonel Norris collected several items from the site, including pottery, a marine shell gorget, and a redstone serpent effigy pipe. These have been curated at the Smithsonian Institution museum since then.

Between 1932 and 1936, an avocational archaeologist and one of the founding members of the West Virginia Archeological Society (WVAS) investigated the Marmet site. Later, other members of the WVAS continued to dig there. Roland Barnett recorded at least fifty burials and many artifacts from Marmet village. Mussel shell from the river was common at the site, representing a local food source and allowing for good preservation of artifacts and remains. In the 1955 *West Virginia Archeologist*, Barnett described a "large ash pit" filled with mussel shell, animal bone and broken pottery sherds. The burial of a woman with 153 glass and shell beads was also found here.[203]

Between 1969 and 1972, WVAS member Hillis Youse visited the Marmet village often. The village site contains a midden layer about thirty inches thick with camp debris from the settlement. In the midden were found animal bone fragments, mussel shell, chert flakes, pottery sherds and fire-cracked rock and charcoal. Ten burials were found below the midden layer in the sandy clay subsoil. There were few items buried with these individuals.[204]

One group of three individuals who were buried together appeared to be a family group who died together. One was a newborn infant who was buried with shell and glass beads and a small spoon made of brass from a European kettle. Two adults were buried with the infant. One of the adults was buried with several items, including pieces of turtle shell, mussel shell, animal bone, pottery sherds and human teeth. The other adult was buried with a pair of mussel shells at the knees and a pair of cylindrical shell pendants below the ears. On the chest of the individual was a cluster of twelve triangular arrow points. In the chest cavity was the tip of a triangular point, possibly indicating an enemy attack.[205]

A large, shell-tempered pottery rim sherd with a corncob-impressed neck from Marmet village. *Grave Creek Mound Archaeological Complex, West Virginia Division of Culture and History.*

Pottery

Pottery from the Marmet village was plentiful. Most was shell tempered with a range of surface treatments. Like many other Fort Ancient villages in West Virginia, pottery vessels exhibited plain, cordmarked, corncob-impressed and mixed surface treatments.[206]

Lithic Materials

Triangular arrow points made from locally available Kanawha Black chert were also plentiful. Other stone items included a turtle effigy made of red shale and a small round discoidal made of sandstone. A stone smoking pipe was also found. Fire-cracked rocks were plentiful from fire hearths used for cooking.[207]

Animal Bone and Bone Tools

Animal bone found at the site included deer, bear, elk and turtle, as well as birds and fish. Animal bone tools were also found, including awls, a drift pin and a bone beamer.[208]

Marine Shell

Marine shell ornaments were common at Marmet village, indicating trade with other Indian groups in the Southeast. At least seven marine shell ornaments were found at the Marmet site. Two were large Buffalo-style engraved shell masks with a Weeping Eye design. These were found during the construction of houses in the residential area of Marmet. One was found on the chest of an adult man. Other marine shell masks and maskettes were found, as well as three round shell gorgets. One is the previously mentioned gorget collected by Colonel Norris in the 1880s. Another round shell gorget recovered exhibited faint markings of a Citico-style rattlesnake design, although the surface is covered by a mineral or organic residue obscuring the faint engravings.[209]

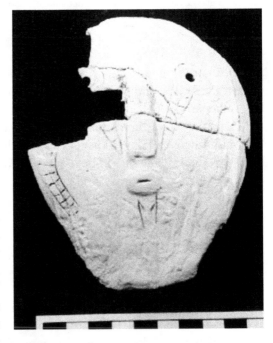

An engraved marine shell mask gorget with the Weeping Eye design from Marmet village. *Blennerhassett Museum.*

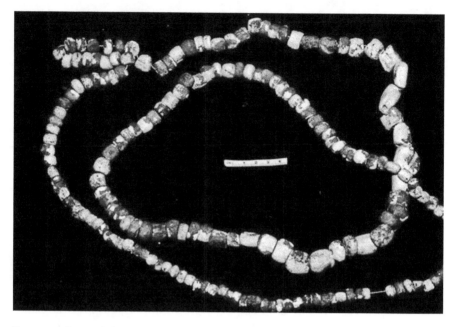

European glass trade beads from Marmet village. *Robert Maslowski.*

Trade Items

European trade goods found at the site included brass from kettles and glass trade beads, indicating Late Fort Ancient period of occupation.[210] No radiocarbon dates are available for the Marmet village, although the European trade items found there place it in the Late Fort Ancient Protohistoric period. The Marmet village is thought to have been one of the latest occupied village sites in the Kanawha Valley prior to its abandonment by AD 1700.

THE MILLER SITE (46JA55)

The Miller site is located on a terrace of the Ohio River a half mile north of Ravenswood in Jackson County, West Virginia, on an alluvial bottom known as Ravenswood Bottom. The bottom contains a lower and a higher terrace, and the Miller site is located on a remnant of the higher terrace.[211]

In 1976, artifacts from the site were brought to the attention of archaeologists at the West Virginia Geological and Economic Survey

(WVGS). At the time, the site was scheduled for destruction by house construction, and therefore, test excavations were arranged by the WVGS to determine the significance of the site. The first surface survey was not able to delineate the total size of the Miller site, but it did indicate that the site was much smaller than other, previously excavated Fort Ancient sites, such as Buffalo or Mount Carbon.[212]

Excavations at the site began by hand, using shovels to remove the topsoil to reach the subsurface clay. Features were defined with trowels and hoes. After a while, the Ohio River Sand and Gravel Company granted permission for the excavators to use their power equipment, and using a front end loader, the excavators stripped the plow zone away, exposing a large area of the site. The midden layer averaged twelve inches deep. The village midden was relatively shallow, suggesting occupation for a short duration or perhaps seasonal occupation.[213]

The goal of the excavations was to assess the size and structure of the site. Trenching at the southern and central portions of the site revealed what appeared to be a domestic zone. The village was circular, like most Fort Ancient villages, and measured about two hundred square feet. There appeared to be no palisade wall at the site, although according to Wilkins, further excavations might prove otherwise. The domestic zone contained an arc of subsurface pits, fired areas and post molds with a plaza area at the center. There were no discernible house patterns revealed, although the post molds appeared to be concentrated around features.[214]

Twenty-four features were noted just below the plow zone, each consisting of charcoal and burned earth from two to seventeen inches thick. These features did not appear to be prepared fire pits. Few cultural materials were found within the fired areas. Nine oval to circular basin-shaped subsurface pits were discovered, extending two to thirteen inches deep. Two other irregular-shaped pits were found as well. The burial of a child, estimated to be five to ten years old, was found, as was a mass of white ash thought to be a secondary burial.[215]

The Miller site excavations uncovered a small circular Early Fort Ancient village. The excavations failed to recognize any discernible post mold patterns that would make it possible to determine the number, size and internal structure of any houses at the village. However, fired areas, subsurface pits and scattered post molds appeared to be concentrated around a central plaza area, suggesting a typical Fort Ancient village plan.[216]

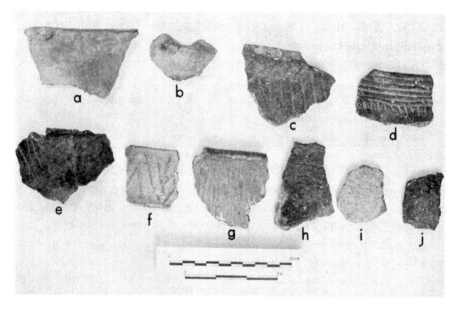

Rim sherds from the Miller site. *Top row*: plain and incised; *bottom row*: incised, cordmarked and knot roughened. *From Wilkins, "Miller Site,"* West Virginia Archeologist.

Pottery

Ceramics found at the Miller site included 1,241 pottery body sherds, 80 rim sherds and 148 unidentifiable sherds for a total of 1,469 pottery sherds. All but 2 were shell tempered, with the remaining 2 being limestone tempered. Most of the pottery was plain, with a few cordmarked and roughened sherds found. Approximately 21.7 percent of the sherds had obviously been cordsmoothed. This occurs when pottery surfaces are cordmarked and then smoothed before firing. This appears to be a common surface treatment from this time.[217]

Plain surfaced pottery was dominant at 79.5 percent, although plain with some decoration accounted for 4.8 percent of body sherds. Cordmarking accounted for 12.5 percent of the assemblage, with 3.2 percent classified as roughened. There were sixty plain body sherds found with incised or punctate decorations. Forty-eight were incised only, ten were with punctates only and two were incised with punctates. Incised designs were predominantly rectilinear, except for two curvilinear examples.[218]

Pottery from the site was light brown to dark gray in color. Rim sherds were vertical to slightly flaring with rounded to flat lips or converging and rounded. Seven of the rims had some decoration. Some rims had appendages attached, including strap handles, semi-lunar lugs, enclosed lugs, spout lugs, noded lugs and mammiform lugs.[219]

Lithic Materials

Over five thousand lithic materials were recovered from the Miller village. The raw material used was mostly from chert pebbles. Another eight pieces were made from quartzite. Colors ranged from gray and bluish brown to yellow. Only sixteen complete triangular points were recovered. The remaining assemblage included projectile point preforms, cores, drills, gravers, bifaces, side scrapers, retouched flakes, hematite, celts and miscellaneous tools.[220]

Faunal Materials

Faunal remains at the Miller site included 2,314 animal bone items. Most of the items (1,951) were from the surface midden. Only features at the site were screened, and fourteen features contained faunal remains. Mammal species found included dog, gray fox, black bear, raccoon, fisher, groundhog, gray squirrel, marsh rice rat, beaver, elk and white-tailed deer. Bird species were wild turkey and duck, and fish found included catfish and sturgeon. Reptiles include box turtles, snapping turtles and spiny softshell turtles. Mussel shells of various species were abundant in the collection and were probably gathered from the nearby river.[221]

Compared to other Fort Ancient sites, the Miller site faunal assemblage shows little diversity, probably due to the small sample size. Elk and deer no doubt provided the largest amounts of meat. No plant remains were recovered, so it is uncertain if the inhabitants of the Miller site engaged in maize agriculture.[222]

Bone Tools

Bone tools and ornaments recovered included four bone splinter awls, three small mammal ulna awls, two deer ulna awls, one deer rib awl, seven bird bone beads, one mammal bone bead, five deer antler projectile tips, one bone drift, one bone needle, three pieces of worked turtle carapace, one scraper with a blunt end and one unidentified tool with a pronged end.[223]

Radiocarbon Dates

One radiocarbon date was obtained from a feature at the Miller site. The resulting date reported was AD 1100.[224] The date would place the Miller village in the Early Fort Ancient period.

MOUNT CARBON VILLAGE (46FA7)

The Mount Carbon village site is located three and a half miles southeast of Montgomery, West Virginia, on the southwest bank of the Kanawha River in Fayette County. The site is located on one of the highest areas in the alluvial bottom and seldom floods. Mount Carbon has been known as an archaeological site since the 1800s, when a railroad spur was cut from Armstrong Creek to the Kanawha River. At that time, thirty burials were noted, along with projectile points, greenstone celts, "quoit-shaped" stones, shell-tempered pottery and bone tools.[225]

More of the site was removed when fill material was cut and used for tamping explosives for nearby coal mines. More burials were found at this time. As a result, local collectors began digging at the site, and much of the village was disturbed.[226]

The Mount Carbon site also appears to have had earlier Adena, Middle Woodland and Late Woodland occupations, as indicated by the recovery of grit-tempered, clay-tempered and shell-tempered pottery.[227] In addition, a fluted point was earlier found at the site by a collector that suggested a very early Paleo-Indian occupation. The point was made from nonlocal chert, possibly from New York Onondaga chert, according to McMichael.[228] The fluted point was found in the burial of a Fort Ancient individual who had probably collected the point and kept it until his death. Several collections of burials and associated materials were reported at different locations, some taken out of West Virginia.[229]

In 1961, because of the previous digging at the site, Dr. Edward McMichael with the West Virginia Geological and Economic Survey (WVGS) began excavations to salvage as much of the site as possible. Two ten-foot squares were first excavated and then another two with laborers from the Aid to Dependent Children Program. Artifacts had been widely scattered by the previous pot hunting. Because much of the village site was damaged, one badly disturbed area was removed by mechanical means.[230]

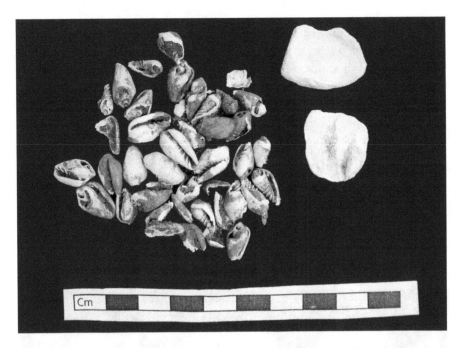

Marginella marine and mussel shells from Mount Carbon village. *Grave Creek Mound Archaeological Complex, West Virginia Division of Culture and History.*

Three palisade lines were found that are thought to be from the Fort Ancient occupation. The palisade walls appeared to have what McMichael interpreted as bastions or small outward projections of the wall. Rectilinear house patterns were also uncovered that appeared to be from the Fort Ancient occupation. Houses measured fifteen by thirteen feet, fifteen by ten and a half feet and thirteen by ten feet in area.[231]

Although only about one-fourth of the village was excavated during the 1961–62 excavations, thirty-seven burials were encountered, some damaged by prior disturbance. One of the burials was inside a house. Burial position was predominantly flexed, and the burial population included seven infants, twelve children, two adolescents, two young adults, six adults and eight mature adults. More than 40 percent of the burials were interred with items, including smoking pipes, pottery vessels, turtle shell cups, projectile points, rolled copper hair tubes, a seed pearl, Marginella shell beads and mussel shell.[232]

No analysis of the copper hair tubes was conducted to see if it was of European origin, and it may have been native copper. No obvious European trade items were recovered, suggesting a pre-contact occupation for the Fort Ancient village.[233]

The most common features found at Mount Carbon were pits. Eighty-two pits were given feature numbers. Most were determined to be from the Fort Ancient occupation and included sixty-one circular, straight-walled flat-bottomed pits. The remainder were deeper, slightly bell-shaped circular pits. These pits contained debris and animal bone, pottery, chert and shell. Forty-one additional pits that contained very little material were uncovered that were thought to be earlier than Fort Ancient.[234]

Pottery

Several types of pottery vessels were found at Mount Carbon that appeared to represent different occupations from the Early Woodland to the Late Prehistoric. Shell-tempered jars were the most common ceramics found

Shell-tempered incised pottery sherds from Mount Carbon. *Grave Creek Mound Archaeological Complex, West Virginia Division of Culture and History.*

at the Fort Ancient component, as well as a few bowls. Pottery vessels had constricted necks and everted rims with round to semiconical bottoms, and some had strap or loop handles. Pottery from the Fort Ancient occupation with a variety of surface treatments was recovered. The most common surface treatment was cordmarking. Other surface treatments included plain, simple stamped (also known as grooved paddle), checked stamped and net impressed. There was also punctation or incising found on plain or smoothed necks of some vessels. McMichael described the Fort Ancient pottery types as Madisonville cordmarked, Madisonville plain, Madisonville grooved paddle, Fox Farm check stamped and Madisonville net impressed.[235]

Lithic Materials

Lithic materials were found from several of the components at Mount Carbon. From the Fort Ancient occupation, triangular bifaces (arrow points) were the most common. Several chert drills and stone scrapers were also recovered. Chipped celts manufactured from local Kanawha Black chert were the most common chopping tool found. Other stone artifacts that were recovered included a few small diamond-shaped pendants from cannel coal and siltstone. Discoidals were also recovered made primarily from sandstone. Several smoking pipes and pipe fragments were also recovered: one vasiform pipe made from sandstone, several pipe stems and an elbow pipe from soapstone (steatite) and a bird effigy pipe made of soft limestone, found with a burial. The latter pipe was covered with organic stains and was incised on both sides.[236]

In a pit in the Fort Ancient component, the so-called Mount Carbon Tablet was found. The "tablet" was manufactured from black slate with one squared end and the other end chipped and rounded. The tablet exhibits faint engraved lines on one side. The pattern of lines appears to be three long lines along the length of the object with shorter perpendicular intersecting lines at regular intervals.[237]

Bone Tools

Abundant bone tools were found at Mount Carbon that McMichael attributed to the Fort Ancient occupation. Tools made from animal bones include bone beamers from white-tailed deer, bears, mountain lions and elk.

Bone awls found were from deer, raccoons, bears, turkeys and unidentified mammals.[238] There were also antler-tip projectile points, antler and bone drifts, antler-tip flakers for flaking stone tools, bone flakers, cut bear teeth, perforated canine teeth from various animals, many turtle shell cups, bird bone beads, bone tubes, one bone needle, bone fishhooks, small bone pins, elk antler hoes (or chisels) and a cut and perforated deer toe bone.[239]

Faunal Remains

Faunal remains found at Mount Carbon were primarily from the Fort Ancient occupation thought to date from AD 1400 to 1500. A total of 18,448 pieces of animal bone were recovered during the 1961 and 1962 excavations. Of these, 11,200 were able to be identified and represented 514 animals. These included 56 vertebrate species, of which 59 percent were mammals, 8 percent were birds, 19 percent were reptiles, less than 1 percent were amphibians and 4 percent were fish.[240]

The variety of the species found indicated a year-round occupation of the village. Species represented were wolf, dog, gray fox, bear, raccoon, bobcat, mountain lion, rice rat, beaver, white-tailed deer, elk, turkey, map turtle, slider turtle, softshell turtle and box turtle.[241]

NEALE'S LANDING (46WD39)

The Neale's Landing and Blennerhassett village sites are both located on Blennerhassett Island in the Ohio River near Parkersburg, Wood County, West Virginia. Neale's Landing is a Protohistoric village located on a bluff or terrace eleven meters from the Ohio River at the maximum island elevation of 604 to 606 feet.[242] This location no doubt offered a defensive advantage. On the north and south sides of Neale's Landing were bluffs more than 30 feet high and active river channels. The settlement was protected on the eastern side by a narrow bluff and a low narrow "neck" of land. Hemmings described the site of Neale's Landing as "a promontory as it is today, but less accessible and more isolated by relief and by river channels." The village itself was surrounded by a palisade.[243]

Early Investigations

Like many known Native American sites in West Virginia, Neale's Landing had been investigated earlier by avocational archaeologists. Dr. Samuael P. Hildreth, a distinguished historian from Ohio, stated, "I once saw a perfect vessel of this [shell-tempered] kind; it would hold about two quarts, was handsomely proportioned, nearly the shape of a large coca-nut, and had four neat handles placed near the brim, opposite to each other. It was found in the bank on an island in the Ohio river near Belpe."[244]

Another collector, Professor Henry Stahl from Parkersburg, West Virginia, collected thousands of artifacts from Blennerhassett Island over the years. According to labeling with his collection, these were collected primarily between 1860 and 1923, when he passed away. However, none of the artifacts is identified by site, making their provenience uncertain.[245]

Another published account of investigations on Blennerhassett Island was by J.P. MacLean in 1884 and titled "Remains on Blennerhassett Island, Ohio River." MacLean had written articles on the mound builders and other topics. He collected hundreds of artifacts from the site and was asked to write an article by Professor Spencer F. Baird of the Smithsonian Institution.[246]

MacLean's description of Neale's Landing reads:

> *The first point examined was the largest shell heap on the island near the center. The deposit is 1,125 feet long....Save along the margin of the bank the shell heap has been plowed over for the last 40 years or more.... Along this bank were made seven excavations; the first was at the eastern extremity....The ridge here is...extremely narrow....It should be remarked that the above excavations did not partake of the true character which that word necessarily implies....Only a few inches along the face of the bank were removed....It is along this bank where most of the implements which have been thrown upon the market have been taken....It is probable that the large [shell heap] faced both shores originally.*[247]

Another archaeological collection from Blennerhassett Island that has been of some scientific value was that collected between 1910 and 1960 by Henry Kelly of Parkersburg. The collection had been catalogued by site, and it was later donated to the West Virginia Archeological Society (WVAS).[248]

Professional Excavations

Throughout the nineteenth and early twentieth centuries, many burials had been exposed by erosion of the island. In the early 1970s, work began through West Virginia's professional archaeology program at the West Virginia Geological and Economic Survey (WVGS) to attempt to salvage what remained of a very important site.[249] Professional excavations began on Blennerhassett Island in the summer of 1973. Tests at Neale's Landing located three human burials. The site was thought at this time to be a cemetery. Further excavations in 1974 uncovered a small permanent settlement with human burials surrounded by living and work areas on the bluff. The site was named "Neale's Landing" after the place name of an adjacent beach, which had long been an accessible landing spot for equipment and farm animals by island farmers.[250]

The objectives of the excavations were to recover as much of the site as possible and determine the nature of the Fort Ancient settlement. The site also had an earlier Woodland component, although there was insufficient evidence of that occupation. At the time of the excavations, the site had been damaged by bank erosion, agricultural activity and unauthorized digging for many years, as well as natural processes.[251]

Results of the excavations indicated that the major Fort Ancient occupation at Neale's Landing was between AD 1500 and 1680.[252] Unlike most Fort Ancient villages that were circular or oval surrounded by a central plaza, the settlement on Blennerhassett Island appeared to be restricted to a linear landform at the "Narrows" of the island. The east–west size of the settlement was probably slightly larger than 400 feet, and the north–south dimension was probably around 150 feet. However, there is evidence of erosion at the site, and earlier accounts suggested a greater size.[253]

The Neale's Landing Fort Ancient component contained three rectangular houses, outdoor work areas and storage facilities located around an open plaza. The occupation covered between one and two acres in a linear pattern surrounded by bluffs. A line of post molds that ran parallel to the riverbank suggested a palisade wall thought to have surrounded the site. The posts were set about one foot apart and were about 0.29 feet in diameter. A gap in the post molds around 3.50 feet wide was probably the entrance to the village, unlike the opening formed by overlapping palisade lines at some villages.[254]

Among the forty features uncovered at the site there were storage pits, outdoor hearths and food preparation areas and five bowl-shaped smudge pits filled with a charred combination of wood charcoal, bark, nutshell and corncobs with a small amount of wood ash, animal remains and inorganic material. Hemmings suggested these pits might have been used for protection from insects or for smoking animal hides.[255] Unlike some other Fort Ancient villages, there was no evidence of refuse disposal areas (middens) around the periphery of the village. Instead, it appeared that large storage pits were filled with refuse.[256]

The best-preserved house pattern (House 1) at the site was rectangular with a curved end wall. This house pattern included sixty-seven post molds representing wall posts set about one foot apart with an interior partition or roof support posts. The floor of the house had been previously removed by plowing, although three sub-floor storage pits remained fairly intact. In addition, there was a short interior partition wall positioned parallel to the east–west axis of the house, and some support posts and posts were associated with storage pits.[257]

Burials

Neale's Landing was long known locally as an Indian cemetery. Thirty-two human burials were found in twenty-seven graves at the village, all attributed to the Fort Ancient component. It was suggested that Neale's Landing was home to three extended families of eight or more individuals living in three houses. About half of the individuals found had associated antler, bone or shell items with them, although, because of poor preservation at the site, some of the items, as well as the remains, were in poor condition. The graves were interspersed among the living and work areas, although the central plaza area contained no burials.[258]

The most frequent body position among primary interments was extended (77 percent), with 29 percent semiflexed. One burial was fully flexed. Two individuals appeared to be situations where the burial was disturbed and then reburied. Burial position was primarily with head to the east-southeast.[259]

Fifty-three percent of the interred individuals were buried with grave items.[260] Several individuals were buried with what might be considered status items. One child of about three years old was buried with a marine shell mask gorget with a Weeping Eye design, a vulture effigy pipe and a pottery jar, among other items. The number and types of items suggested some sort of ascribed rank. Several infants were buried with pottery vessels. One young adult female was buried with a blue glass trade bead. This was the only instance of a European trade item found among the burials. In addition, several adult men showed evidence of enemy attacks in the form of embedded arrows; one contained eighteen.[261]

Lithic Material

Lithic materials from the Neale's Landing Fort Ancient village included 859 triangular points, 246 triangular performs, 105 endscrapers, seventy-nine flake cutting tools, seventy-two ovoid performs, sixty-two indeterminate bifaces, fifty-four drills, fourteen special bifaces, thirteen flake scraping tools and seven heavy-duty cutting tools. A total of seventy-two triangular points was found with burials and victims of arrow wounds.[262]

A total of 80.5 kilograms of chert cores and debitage was collected from the site. The large sample indicates fairly intensive lithic workshop activity, much of it for projectile point manufacture. The suggestion was that the raw material from the site was overwhelmingly obtained from local river gravels, such as chert and jasper pebbles. Only traces of imported cherts, such as Kanawha Black chert and Flint Ridge chert, were represented. The pebble flint primarily used for flint knapping at Neale's Landing varied from black or blue-gray to lighter shades of gray and creamy tan.[263]

Ground stone tools from the village consisted of twenty-nine hammerstones, nineteen palettes (primarily fragments), eleven celts and adzes, eight grinding slabs, eight pitted cobbles, five abraders, four whetstones, three celt/adze performs, two manos and one pitted slab or anvil. Most of the tools were made from natural pebbles, cobbles or boulders.[264]

Smoking Pipes

Both stone and ceramic smoking pipes were recovered from the Fort Ancient component at Neale's Landing. Eight smoking pipes were recovered from the Fort Ancient component at Neale's Landing during the 1970s excavations. These included three ceramic pipes—one an elbow pipe and two fragments. Stone pipes from the site consisted of two pipe fragments made from calcite, two vasiform pipes—one from fireclay and one from limestone—and one excellent black vulture effigy pipe from fireclay.[265]

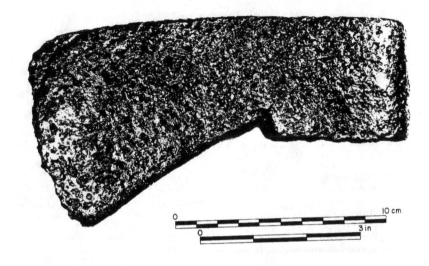

An iron trade axe from Neale's Landing. *West Virginia Archeological Society, Baker 1984.*

European Trade Items

In addition to the glass bead found with a burial, a European iron axe and glass beads were found with the village refuse in a small basin-shaped hearth. The hearth also contained a simple-stamped pottery sherd, a triangular biface fragment and other tools and shell-tempered ceramics mixed with food remains. The iron axe is thought to be a French-type axe similar to those associated with the French fur trade.[266] Similar iron axes have been found at the Late Fort Ancient Rolf Lee village and in a stone mound burial of an adolescent in Mason County.[267]

Pottery

A total of 2,847 whole pottery vessels and sherds was recovered from Neale's Landing village. All were shell tempered, and approximately 33.4 percent were cordmarked. Another 33.3 percent of the assemblage exhibited a simple-stamped surface treatment and applied rim strips similar to Wellsburg-type vessels from the Muskingum Valley. Similar pottery vessels have been found at the Fort Ancient Orchard site in Mason County.

A Wellsburg-style pottery vessel with an applied rim strip from Neale's Landing. *Grave Creek Mound Archaeological Complex, West Virginia Division of Culture and History.*

Stanley Baker conducted the ceramic analysis of the Neale's Landing pottery assemblage. Using whole and reconstructed vessels, Baker analyzed the vessel form, appendages, surface treatment and decorative detailing of thirty-three complete or reconstructed pottery vessels.[268]

The results of Baker's analysis indicated that three major types of ceramic jars, one atypical jar and one bowl were present at Neale's Landing in the plow zone, in feature fill, with burials and in burial fill. The three predominant types were typical Fort Ancient Madisonville ceramics, Wellsburg ceramic types and a new Neale's Landing type.[269]

Madisonville ceramics consisted of ten vessels, or 30.2 percent of the assemblage. Although the type was not the most common, it was well represented. The ten vessels recovered were very similar to those from the original Madisonville site in Ohio. Madisonville ceramics from Neale's Landing exhibited the low globular body, constricted neck and flaring rim characteristic of the type. Four of the Madisonville pottery vessels at Neale's Landing were cordmarked below the neck, and two were simple-stamped. Four were undetermined.[270]

Wellsburg-type ceramics were the most common type at Neale's Landing with eleven complete vessels, or 33.3 percent of the assemblage, analyzed. They were indistinguishable from certain vessel types found in the Muskingum Valley in Ohio. Wellsburg pottery vessels are typically simple stamped, although cordmarked types also occur. At Neale's Landing, five vessels were simple-stamped, and three were cordmarked. All of the surfaces of the Wellsburg ceramics had been wiped before firing to varying degrees. The surface of another simple-stamped vessel was so eroded as to appear plain. Two vessels had undetermined surfaces.[271]

The Neale's Landing site is the type-site for a stylistically distinct group of pottery vessels named, appropriately, Neale's Landing. This type of pottery vessel accounted for eight vessels, or 24.2 percent of the pottery assemblage. They have been found at other sites but were not defined as a type until the work at Neale's Landing. The Neale's Landing type is represented by a low globular or possibly elongate globular jar form with a slightly constricting neck and nearly straight or slightly inverted rim. The vessels are typically simple stamped and marked with shallow, closely spaced grooves. Wiping of the surface while the vessel was still in a plastic state was noted and partially masked the impressions. The vessels are nearly all shoulderless.[272]

Seven pottery vessels were found with burials. Of those seven, five were with children or fetuses, and one was with a female. The remaining Wellsburg-style vessel was found in a burial pit with no human remains.[273]

Wellsburg vessels from burials at Neale's Landing lacked sooting on the exterior surface, unlike similar vessel rims found in refuse pits. This suggests that special funerary jars may have been made for interment with certain individuals. In addition, the volume of Wellsburg vessels from burials ranged from 0.5 to 0.8 liters, making them unsuitable for cooking use.[274] By comparison, Madisonville vessels do not exhibit a similar range in size, and sooting does occur on both jars found with burials at Neale's Landing, as well as those found in refuse pits.[275]

The relative location of Blennerhassett Island and Neale's Landing between the Fort Ancient Madisonville village to the west and Wellsburg peoples to the north, in addition to the similar predominance of Fort Ancient Madisonville and Wellsburg types of pottery, suggests intensive interactions—perhaps intermarriage—between the inhabitants of Neale's

Landing village and both Madisonville and Wellsburg phase peoples. It has been suggested both archaeologically and ethnohistorically that pottery was typically produced by women.[276] This would account for at least some of the exotic pottery forms found at many Fort Ancient villages.

Radiocarbon Dates

Four radiocarbon dates were obtained from wood charcoal from the Late Fort Ancient component Neale's Landing village. Dates obtained were AD 1520, plus or minus 75 years; AD 1290, plus or minus 135 years; AD 1580, plus or minus 155 years; and AD 1585, plus or minus 100 years.[277] However, the presence of European glass beads with burials suggests the Fort Ancient occupation extended into the Protohistoric period in the seventeenth century. Hemmings also suggested that the Late Fort Ancient occupation at Neale's Landing was probably between AD 1550 and 1650.[278]

ORCHARD (46MS61)

The Orchard site is located on a second terrace of the Ohio River, about six miles above the mouth of the Kanawha River in Mason County, West Virginia.[279] Most of the site was located in the old orchard on the property that was planted sometime in the 1800s. The site was discovered around 1938, when a young man who lived on the property noticed a fish effigy pipe that had been dug up by a hog and began digging himself. He and several other avocational archaeologists excavated there until World War II, when the U.S. government built a TNT plant on part of the property. Other collectors excavated there until the 1960s.

According to Jeffrey Graybill, the Orchard village was unlike the typical circular Fort Ancient villages surrounded by a palisade but had a dispersed layout more closely related to historic Indian villages of the 1700s.[280]

The topsoil layer at the site contained a dark, rich midden layer, one to two feet thick, while the subsoil was sandy clay. The top midden layer contained mussel shell, animal bones and broken implements. There were also many large ash pits that were excavated. Most of the burials and artifacts were found in the midden layer, although a few burial pits extended into the subsoil. The Orchard site covers about seven acres.[281]

Excavations

Over three hundred burials were reportedly excavated from the Orchard site between 1941 and 1955. The burials were located between one and four feet deep. Of ninety-two burials where position was recorded, 39 percent were fully extended, and 50 percent were flexed or semiflexed. There were also six bundle burials and four individuals (three children and one woman) buried in a sitting position. There was also evidence of hostility, possibly warfare, at the Orchard site, indicated by several individuals with multiple embedded arrow points in them. There were two group burials, one containing about twelve individuals and one containing eight individuals. One reported mass burial contained nearly forty individuals.[282]

The collectors who excavated at Orchard kept thorough notes of their excavations. Many made sketches showing burial position and associated artifacts. However, there were numerous pit features excavated and post molds noted that were not well documented. There is a rough site map showing relative locations of burials in a roughly circular pattern, although there is not enough detail to re-create the village plan with any degree of certainty.

Mortuary Vessels

One of the unique characteristics of the Orchard Site is the large number of burials with mortuary vessels. Over one hundred pottery vessels were found with 25 to 30 percent of the burials.[283] From the burials with records, 17 percent of the vessels were found with men, 31 percent with women and 52 percent with children. Several children were buried with multiple vessels.

Many of the pottery vessels still contained evidence of food.[284] A single mussel shell, presumably used as a spoon, was found with some of the pottery vessels. This high frequency of mortuary vessels is similar to that found at the Madisonville site in Ohio, parts of Hardin village in Kentucky and Neale's Landing in West Virginia.

The pottery found at Orchard represents quite a range of style and treatment. The strongest similarity is with pottery from the Madisonville site in Ohio, although several Wellsburg-type vessels indicate probable interaction with the Riker site in Ohio.

Since ceramics throughout eastern North America were traditionally made and used by women, the presence of exotic pottery styles can be

A plain-surface pottery vessel with two opposing strap handles from the Orchard site. *Roland Barnett.*

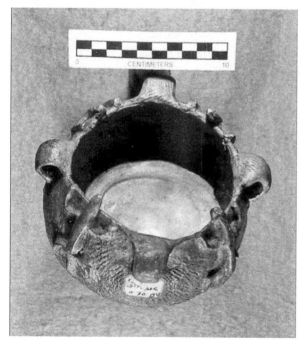

A pottery vessel with lizard effigies around the rim and four strap handles from the Orchard site. *Roland Barnett.*

106

an indicator of movement of women possibly through intermarriage, forced assimilation, exchange of pots or imitation of a new style seen elsewhere.[285]

Smoking Pipes

Smoking pipes were also common at the Orchard site. Over fifty were reported, 91 percent with burials of adult men. This differs from Madisonville, where most pipes were found in cache pits. Pipes were often exchanged between groups during trade to solidify alliances. They were also very personal possessions that were typically buried with their owner.

As with the pots, a variety of styles, decoration and materials were used for smoking pipes that included sandstone, limestone, calcite, catlinite, slate or shale, clay and green and black steatite. Pipe styles found at Orchard include disc, effigy, platform, elbow, vasiform and keel-shaped types. There was also one black steatite elbow pipe with a copper insert. Disc, vasiform and keel-shaped pipes have been found only at sites

Smoking pipes showing a variety of forms and materials from the Orchard site. *Roland Barnett.*

EARLY NATIVE AMERICANS IN WEST VIRGINIA

with Late Fort Ancient components. Orchard is the only Fort Ancient site in West Virginia from which keel-shaped pipes (at least four) have been reported.[286]

Lithic Materials

Triangular arrow points were the most common type of projectile point found at the Orchard site. The bases ranged from straight (about 30 percent) to concave (about 61 percent).[287] Many of the burials also contained bipointed willow leaf-shaped blades, some of which were over six inches long. A couple of Early Archaic Thebes or Kirk-like points were also found, along with triangular points, suggesting the earlier points may have been found by Fort Ancient individuals. Several of the deeper burials contained stemmed points with beveled edges.[288]

Two adult men were buried with what were interpreted as flint knapping toolkits. These included an antler flaking tool, a shaft wrench, abrading stones, antler plugs, projectile point preforms and numerous finished points.

Marine Shell

About 30 percent of the burials at the Orchard site were accompanied by marine shell beads and ornaments. Several types of marine shells were used for necklaces. Several burials were reported with cowrie shell beads, although these were probably Marginella shells. Three burials had marine shell ear ornaments. There were also several individuals found with marine shell gorgets. One infant was found with two small maskettes engraved with the Weeping Eye motif. Another unengraved maskette was found in the burial of a small child that also contained five pottery vessels. Two McBee-style mask gorgets were found at the Orchard site, and a round marine shell gorget was found with very faint rattlesnake engravings.[289]

Bone/Antler Tools and Ornaments

Bone artifacts were plentiful at the Orchard site. Turkey leg bone and deer bone awls were common, as were bone beamers for removing hair from hides, long bone needles, bone tubes, bone fishhooks and bone hair tubes.

Marine shell ornaments from the Orchard site. *Roland Barnett.*

Bone tools from the Orchard site. These include bone awls and scrapers, bone tubes, a bone harpoon and a bone rasp. *Roland Barnett.*

A turtle shell rattle containing pebbles and fish teeth from the Orchard site. *Roland Moxley.*

Deer leg bone beads were also found. At least one bone awl with transverse notching along the spine came from the site, similar to that found at the Madisonville site and several Whittlesey sites in Ohio.[290]

A number of ceremonial or recreational musical instruments, such as bone flutes and at least one bone rasp, were also found. In Fort Ancient territory, bone rasps have been only reported from Protohistoric sites that also contain European materials. One adult male was found with a turtle shell rattle containing seventeen small quartz pebbles and thirty-seven round drum fish teeth.[291]

Two single-barbed antler harpoons were found at the Orchard site. Antler harpoons were found throughout the Great Lakes region.[292] This appears to be the only Fort Ancient site in West Virginia where an antler harpoon has been found, although several were found at the Madisonville village in Ohio.[293]

Fourteen burials contained bone bead skirts usually consisting of several hundred beads made from deer leg bone. One individual was buried with a turkey wing digit skirt. Several burials contained necklaces made from drilled bear, elk or canine teeth.[294]

European metal artifacts from the Orchard site. *Roland Barnett.*

European Trade Items

Metal artifacts were also found with burials at the Orchard site indicating a Protohistoric period of occupation for the Fort Ancient village. Rolled copper or brass beads and tubes, copper or brass tinklers, clips, two copper or brass armbands and a metal dog-head effigy cutout were found.[295]

Two European tubular twisted red glass beads and about forty round blue glass beads were reported from the burial of an infant at the Orchard site.

Status Burials

Several individuals might be considered persons of status in the community from items found buried with them. One adult man was buried with four gorgets, two pendants and ten long shell beads. Also found was a flint knife, two hematite stones and two deer antlers. In his right hand was a limestone platform pipe, around his knees were forty Marginella shell beads and at his right side were thirty-three triangular points in a bundle, as if in a quiver. A large two-lug pot was found on his chest.

Another adult man was reported to have a cut wolf jaw insert in his mouth. His front teeth had been ground to allow the insertion. This type of ceremonial item may have been part of a wolf headdress similar to that usually associated with Adena burials.[296]

One elderly woman was accompanied by six bone tubes, one by six inches long, as well as five bone awls, a bone or antler scraper and two long slender bone needles. The large number of tools suggests she may have been a weaver, worker of hides or perhaps a medicine woman. Several sources have reported bone tubes used by medicine women to symbolically "suck out illness" from patients.[297] The bone awls and needles might have been used either as tattooing instruments or for piercing the skin to allow medicine into the body. Bone needles have also been used in some societies as skewers for piercing the skin.

Several burials were reported to have red or white paint on the remains or burial items. The red and white symbolism of war and peace has been linked to the historic Central Algonquian groups in the Ohio Valley. Several of these indigenous groups used white feathers and other items to decorate peace pipes or other objects while using red paint, clay or markers to decorate war-related pipes and other items.[298]

In 2009, archaeologist Jarrod Burks conducted geophysical survey of two areas at the Orchard site that were thought to possibly be undisturbed. Although the results showed that both areas had been disturbed by utility and drainage lines and ditches and other disturbances, Burks stated that there might still be intact areas and careful excavations might one day produce data that could help better understand the Orchard site.[299]

Radiocarbon Dates

There are two recent radiocarbon dates from corncobs recovered from the Orchard site. The AMS dates from the Illinois Geological Survey are AD 1556–1633 from Feature 26 and AD 1543–1635 from Feature 27.[300]

However, from the artifact assemblage, several preliminary conclusions can be drawn. It appears that there were probably multiple occupations at the site. Multiple occupations at the same site make placing artifacts from specific occupations difficult, especially since the data was collected by amateur archaeologists. Most of the burials and associated artifacts from Orchard appear to be Late Fort Ancient.

The individuals who excavated the Orchard site believed that some of the deeper burials represented an earlier Woodland occupation from the scarcity of burial items and lack of tooth decay. The wolf teeth insert and the deer antler headpiece buried with two adult men are typically Adena ceremonial items. Several stemmed projectile points were found with individuals in the deeper layer as well. The high percentage of flexed and semiflexed burials might also indicate an earlier occupation, as the proportion of extended burials increased through time. There was at least one grit-tempered pot found at Orchard, as well as triangular knives and stone discoidals, which have been found on early Fort Ancient sites in southwestern Ohio.[301]

The metal artifacts and glass beads point to a Late Fort Ancient Protohistoric component as well. Orchard shares many of the characteristics of other Fort Ancient sites, such as Madisonville pottery and Clover bowls. Artifacts such as small disc- and keel-shaped pipes, mushroom-shaped earplugs and marine shell masks and maskettes indicate a Late Fort Ancient Protohistoric occupation.

From the similarity between the assemblages at Madisonville and Orchard, it seems certain that the two villages shared long and continual interaction possibly before and during the Late Fort Ancient period.[302] Like Madisonville, Orchard probably had multiple Fort Ancient occupations, although the use of mortuary vessels probably peaked there during the sixteenth century.

The evidence for interaction between Orchard and the pre-seventeenth century Riker site in Ohio is also plentiful. In addition to the vessels with Wellsburg-style applied rim strips found at the Orchard village, there were other artifacts in common, such as vasiform and keel-shaped pipes and willow leaf blades. The use of mortuary vessels at Riker was common, and there were a large number of burials with pipes.[303] Similarities between the artifact assemblages at Orchard, Madisonville and Riker suggest that the major Orchard site occupation was before AD 1600.

PRATT (46KA31)

The town of Pratt is located on the Kanawha River in Kanawha County, south of Charleston. Originally, the town was called Clifton or Clifton Works. When it was incorporated in 1905, the town was renamed Pratt after the owner of the Charles Pratt Coal Company, Charles Pratt.

In the 1880s, the Bureau of American Ethnology (BAE) of the Smithsonian Institution conducted a series of investigations of burial mounds and known archaeological sites in the Ohio Valley. The results were published in 1894 as the *Report on the Mound Explorations of the Bureau of Ethnology* (BAE) by Cyrus Thomas. Excavations of mounds and other sites in West Virginia were conducted by Colonel P.W. Norris. One of the known sites that were investigated was at Pratt (then known as Clifton Works).[304]

Cyrus Thomas described the "village" of Clifton as located on one of the typical bottoms on the south side of the river and reported that excavations there "seldom fail to bring to light human bones, fragments of pottery,

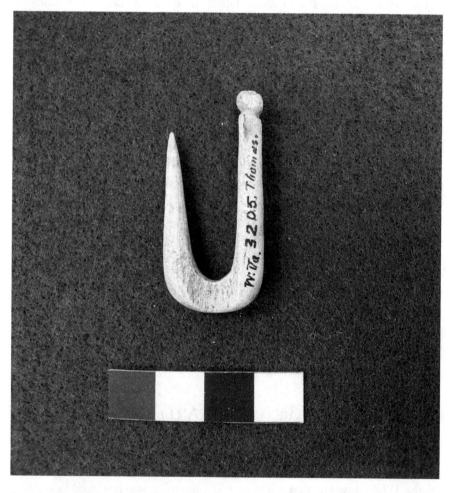

An animal bone fishhook from Pratt (Clifton) now at the Smithsonian Museum (Catalogue No. 87831). *Department of Anthropology, Smithsonian Institution.*

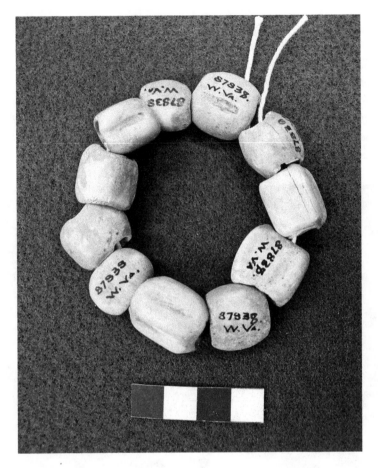

These deer leg bone beads from Pratt (Clifton) are now at the
Smithsonian Museum (Catalogue No. 87838). *Department of Anthropology,
Smithsonian Institution.*

stone implements, and other evidences of previous occupancy."[305] The
BAE excavators spent several days there and reported finding "a marked
uniformity in the earth and its contents."[306] Thomas went on to say, "The
sandy soil, which extends to the depth of 4 and 5 feet, was found to be
literally filled with charcoal, ashes, fragments of pottery, entire and broken
stone implements, etc."[307] He described the site as

*probably a village site or camping ground, occupied continuously, or season
after season for a long time, by a band of aborigines, but so far back in the
past that the entire area was overgrown with the largest timber of the valley
when first visited by white men, nearly a century and a half ago. Comingled*

with these relics, at a depth of from 2 to 4 feet, were found several medium-sized skeletons in various stages of decay. All were lying extended on the back or side, but in no regular order in respect to each other or the points of the compass. With some of these were quite a number of large beads (probably used as rattles), made by cutting short sections of the leg bones of small animals and the bones of birds. These, one bone fishhook, and several bone bodkins, found near the surface, are but slightly decayed, and are probably the work of Indians.[308]

Two Citico-style rattlesnake engraved marine gorgets from Pratt. *David Martin.*

Like many other Fort Ancient village sites in West Virginia, the site at Pratt was never formally investigated.

In the 1930s, during the construction of the Pratt City Hall, several artifacts were uncovered. Two Citico-style rattlesnake marine shell gorgets and a bone hairpin were given to Leslie Martin, a local amateur archaeologist.

ROLF LEE (46MS51)

The Rolf Lee site is located on the Rolf Lee farm on the Ohio River about seven miles south of Point Pleasant, in Mason County, West Virginia. The village site is a Late Fort Ancient Protohistoric-period site. For many years the site was a favorite of local collectors who surface-hunted and dug there with the permission of the owner, Mr. Rolf Lee. The village site has never been systematically investigated. The archaeological site covers an area from the Ohio River to the surrounding hills and is bisected by WV Route 2.[309]

The Protohistoric Rolf Lee site has two site numbers, 46MS51 and 46MS123, and according to Jeffrey Graybill, the site may have contained two overlapping villages occupied at different times. These are designated as Rolf Lee 1 and 2. Graybill thought that Rolf Lee 2 was occupied before Rolf Lee 1, based on his frequency seriation of ceramic surface treatments. However, Graybill noted that there were problems with the seriation and that the treatment ordered sites in a general way only.[310]

In 1964, Mr. Rolf Lee entered into a lease agreement with members of the Kanawha Chapter of the West Virginia Archeological Society (WVAS), giving them permission to excavate at the site. The purpose of the excavation was to determine who the predominant occupants of the site were and if they were Fort Ancient as previously thought.[311]

The area selected for excavation was about one hundred square feet near the riverbank. The area was divided into squares and given letter and number designations. Twenty-eight squares were excavated at random to provide a representative sample of the site.[312]

The plow zone was about eight to nine inches deep and contained an abundance of mussel shell from the river, as well as animal bone, fire-cracked rock, flint chips, triangular arrow points and shell-tempered pottery sherds. Seven or eight inches beneath the plow zone layer, the soil was nearly as dark and contained the same kinds of materials but with less frequency. Below these layers, the soil became increasingly lighter in color and nearly sterile except for post molds, pits, burials and a few artifacts. At around twenty-six to twenty-eight inches below the surface, the soil became a light-brown "hard pan" with only a few burials, post molds and pits.[313]

One refuse pit, about eighteen by twenty-four inches in plan and eighteen inches deep, contained pottery sherds, deer bone, a broken stone celt, ashes and charcoal. The material recovered was considered Fort Ancient in time. Thirty-two post molds were also uncovered. The post molds did not form any recognizable pattern because of the limited excavations conducted.[314]

The burials of nineteen individuals and additional fragmentary remains of other individuals were uncovered at the Rolf Lee village during the excavations. Some appeared to have been possibly disturbed by earlier excavations and others by plowing at the farm. At least fourteen of the individuals appeared to have a general eastern orientation.[315]

One adult man appeared to have died from arrow wounds, with five associated triangular arrow points and a wound in the upper leg bone that matched the broken end of one of the points. Several other individuals were interred together and appeared to be family members.[316]

Pottery

Nearly all of the pottery found at Rolf Lee was shell tempered, except for five small pieces that were tempered with crushed rock or clay. No complete pottery vessels were recovered. Strap handles were more common than lugs on the pottery recovered. Pottery rims were plain, notched, serrated, fingernail impressed or scalloped, and a few rims had a notched thickened lip or a notched fillet below the lip.[317]

One piece of pottery that might have been a lug handle from a vessel appeared to represent the head of a fish with an open eye on one side and closed eye on the other side. A clay pipe with a broken stem in the shape of half a walnut shell was also found, as well as a clay effigy of a woman from the waist up about two inches long. The head had been broken off. In addition, the body of an unbaked clay doll about six inches long was found with a discoidal on top of it.[318]

Pottery from the Rolf Lee village site included a variety of surface treatments. These include cordmarked, plain, knotted net impressed and corncob impressed. There were also several pottery sherds with an unknown surface treatment that resembled a basket weave.[319]

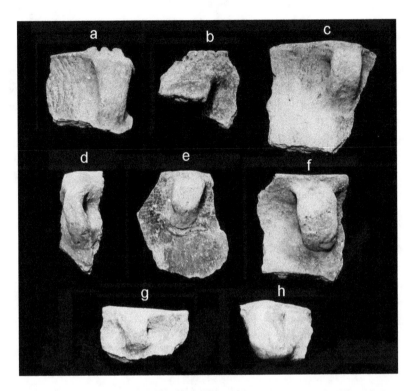

Rim sherds with strap handles and assorted surface treatments from Rolf Lee. *Grave Creek Mound Archaeological Complex, West Virginia Division of Culture and History.*

Pottery sherds with knotted net impressing from Rolf Lee. *Grave Creek Mound Archaeological Complex, West Virginia Division of Culture and History.*

Lithic Materials

Several worked stone implements were found, including celts; a stone hoe; a pestle; a large, flat cupped stone; and a round grinding stone. Engraved pieces of cannel coal were also found. Flint or chert was mostly Kanawha Black chert, probably from local river cobbles. Projectile points were mostly triangular arrow points, frequently with a concave base, although one willow leaf blade was also found, as were a few earlier notched points. Teardrop-shaped thumbnail scrapers were found, as well as flint drills, hammerstones, a stone hoe, a pestle and a grinding stone.[320]

Faunal Remains

Most of the animal bone found at Rolf Lee was from white-tailed deer. Also found were bear and wolf teeth. There were turkey bones found, as well as turtle and fish bones and fish scales. Mussel shells were also recovered throughout the midden layer.[321]

Bone Tools and Ornaments

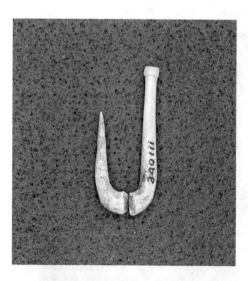

Some of the animal bone had been worked into tools, including awls, antler flaking tools, a weaving tool, a scraper, two antler-tip projectile points, a bone fishhook and a bone hairpin. Deer bone beads and animal canine pendants and beads were also found: one from a bear, two from wolves and four from smaller animals. At least one bone flute was found, possibly from a turkey leg bone.[322]

Bone fishhook from Rolf Lee (Catalogue No. 340111). *Department of Anthropology, Smithsonian Institution.*

Animal canine teeth from Rolf Lee (Catalogue No. A340115). *Department of Anthropology, Smithsonian Institution.*

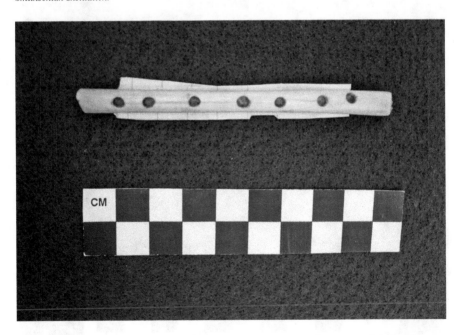

An animal bone flute from Rolf Lee (Catalogue No. A340112). *Department of Anthropology, Smithsonian Institution.*

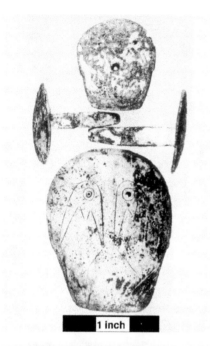

1 inch

Left: A marine shell maskette, ear ornaments and an engraved mask gorget with Weeping Eye design from the Rolf Lee site. *Bill Williams*.

Below: A marine shell mask with Weeping Eye design from Rolf Lee. *Harvey Allen*.

Marine Shell

Marine shell was abundant at Rolf Lee and was represented by Marginella shell in the form of necklaces and bracelets. Many marine shell items accompanied the individuals interred at the Rolf Lee village. One child about six years old was accompanied by about 350 small disc beads and small shell and glass trade beads around his/her neck. Two small bracelets accompanied an infant. These contained forty-six tubular shell beads. An adolescent boy was accompanied by fifty shell beads behind his head as if they had been worn in his hair. An adult woman wore a string of mixed tubular and Marginella shell beads around her neck. One child between the ages of five and ten wore a string of small shell beads, one glass trade bead and a small shell disc gorget around his/her neck.[323]

Rolf Lee contained the largest number of marine shell gorgets recorded at a known Fort Ancient site in West Virginia, with at least twenty-six found. These consisted of thirteen marine shell masks, four rattlesnake gorgets, six small shell maskettes, two plain gorgets and one reported spider gorget, although the whereabouts of the spider gorget remains unknown.[324]

European Trade Items

The Rolf Lee village produced more European trade items than any other site in West Virginia.[325] European trade items recovered from Rolf Lee included European glass beads and copper and/or brass tubular beads and small flat metal pieces cut into several shapes. Several large brass arm bands were found that were obviously made from brass kettles and still exhibited the rivets used for attaching handles.[326] The brass and/or copper items and European glass beads at Rolf Lee indicated trade with native peoples in the East in contact with European groups. The location of the site on the Ohio River about five miles below the mouth of Kanawha River placed it near the junction of two major trade routes.

Hundreds of European glass trade beads were found with burials at Rolf Lee. Stanley Baker (1986) noted that the types of beads and their frequencies were similar to collections of trade beads found on Protohistoric sites in Pennsylvania and suggested that their occurrence would date the Rolf Lee village to the 1600s. He also stated that the most likely source for the glass trade beads found at Rolf Lee and other Fort Ancient sites in the Upper

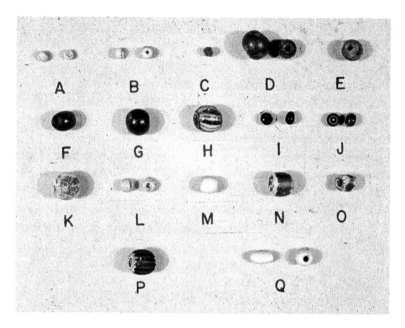

European glass trade beads from Rolf Lee. *Grave Creek Mound Archaeological Complex, West Virginia Division of Culture and History.*

European brass or copper tubular beads and tinklers from Rolf Lee (Catalogue No. 340118). *Department of Anthropology, Smithsonian Institution.*

Ohio Valley would have been the Susquehannock people in the Eastern Panhandle and Pennsylvania.[327]

The Protohistoric Late Fort Ancient Rolf Lee village is thought by some archaeologists to have been the last Native American village occupied in West Virginia before Europeans entered the Kanawha Valley. The one calibrated radiocarbon date for the site is AD 1666.[328]

ROSEBERRY FARM AND MOUND (46MS53)

Roseberry Farm is an Early Fort Ancient village with an associated burial mound located on a high terrace about three-tenths of a mile from the Ohio River in Mason County along a tributary stream called Old Town Creek. Old Town Creek was named for a reported Indian village there that has never been located. Paleo-Indian and Archaic points have been found on this terrace, indicating its use for at least ten thousand years. Roseberry Farm is a very early Fort Ancient period site dating from AD 1010 to 1270.[329]

The Roseberry Farm site was first recorded in 1953 by Leonard Johnson, who was under contract with the West Virginia Archeological Society (WVAS). No excavations were conducted at that time, but a small surface collection suggested a Fort Ancient village at this location. Subsequently, the site was tested in 1976 to establish the age of the village, its condition and possible cultural affiliation. These tests revealed a Fort Ancient presence and traces of earlier Woodland occupations.[330]

Between 1976 and 1978, the site was excavated on three occasions by archaeologists from the West Virginia Geological and Economic Survey (WVGS). The 1976 excavations were conducted to determine the physical condition of the site and its age and possible cultural affiliation. At this time, two small trenches were dug along the western edge of the site. These excavations documented a Fort Ancient component, as well as traces of earlier occupations. More extensive excavations were conducted in 1977 and 1978, when the property was purchased for development. The new owner of the property had plans to level the mound to build a house. These were salvage excavations to obtain as much information as possible about the site before its destruction.[331]

Excavations at the village site revealed an Early Woodland occupation with Adena plain pottery sherds and a Middle Woodland component with Watson cordmarked pottery and Fairchance and Jacks Reef projectile

125

points. This Middle Woodland occupation also included several pit features and a single burial with five projectile points and two abrading stones. The Middle Woodland component overlapped the Fort Ancient village partially, with its greatest concentration along the western portion of the site.[332]

Because Roseberry Farm was a very early Fort Ancient village with a burial mound, Dr. Jeffrey Graybill, the WVGS archaeologist who conducted the excavations, hoped the site might show the early stages of village development and how Late Woodland habitation sites evolved from small hamlets into larger complex Fort Ancient villages. Results of the excavations and the intensity and artifacts from the Middle Woodland period suggested that the Roseberry Farm site was, in fact, a settled habitation area before the Fort Ancient village was constructed, dating between AD 200 and 900.[333]

Radiocarbon dates for the village ranged from AD 1010 to AD 1590, although acceptable dates suggest AD 1010 to AD 1270 as a closer time frame for the village occupation, placing it well within the Early Fort Ancient period.[334]

The Fort Ancient Roseberry Farm village was circular (about ninety meters in diameter) with a central plaza and a burial mound to the west. Early Fort Ancient villages sometimes included burial mounds, although it is very unusual in West Virginia. Around the plaza area was a domestic zone with pit house structures, surface structures, hearths, pits and some burials. Also unusual were the pit house structures found there. Pit houses were dug below the ground surface. These were the first pit houses reported in West Virginia. Pit houses are much more common in the southeastern United States. Jeffrey Graybill has stated that the structures probably occurred at other villages occupied before AD 1450 but were not noted before because early investigators failed to identify them.[335]

There were ten to twenty square or rectangular pit houses partially excavated at the Roseberry Farm village. Only one pit house was thoroughly excavated. The house was surrounded by post molds and measured 14.4 by 21.0 feet, and the house floor was 2.5 feet below the ground surface.[336]

There were two zones at the village. There was the central plaza with the mound to the southwest and an encircling domestic zone with fire pits, storage pits and the pit house structures. There were also burials throughout the village. Unlike later Fort Ancient villages, no evidence of a palisade wall was found.[337]

A large number of household items from everyday life were found. These included objects made from stone, shell, bone and antler, as well as pottery. Projectile points, discoidals, a cannel-coal pendant, smoking pipes, celts and nutting stones were found. A fragment of a stone figure of a woman was also found.[338]

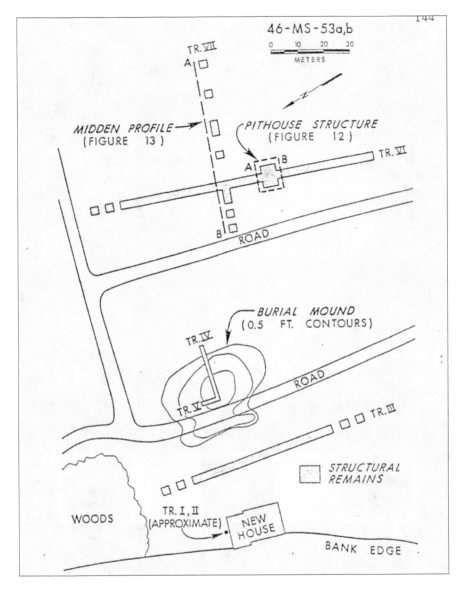

A map of Roseberry Farm showing excavations. *Jeffrey Graybill.*

Pottery from Roseberry Farm was made from locally available clay and tempered with mussel shell. Most were jars with handles and constricted necks. The surfaces were plain, and there were several different types of rims with handles and decorations.

Abundant food remains were found at Roseberry Farm, including animal bone, mussel shell and plants. There were forty or more species of faunal

A pottery rim with incised decoration and strap handle from Roseberry Farm. *Grave Creek Mound Archaeological Complex, West Virginia Division of Culture and History.*

remains found, including white-tailed deer, elk, black bear, wild turkey, raccoon, gray squirrel, box turtle and drum fish. There were also thousands of mussel shells found of various species.[339] Plant remains included maize and other cultivated plants, seeds, nuts and a large charred mass of about nine hundred whole or broken corncobs. The corn mass was thought to be

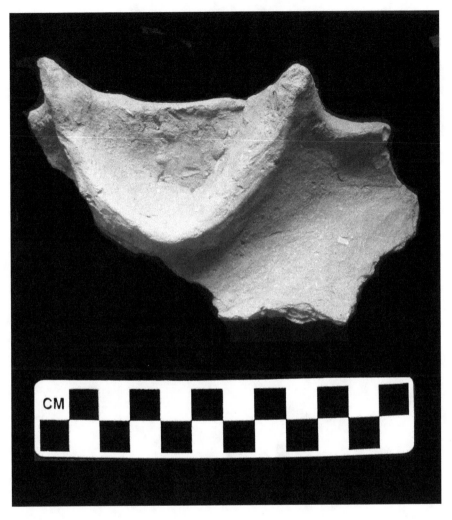

An unusual pottery rim with lug handle from Roseberry Farm. *Grave Creek Mound Archaeological Complex, West Virginia Division of Culture and History.*

from a pit. The corn was all eastern eight-row or northern flint corn, early strains of corn.[340]

The Roseberry Farm Mound was about two feet tall and sixty feet in diameter. It was located within the village between the central plaza and the domestic zones. From the small area of the mound that was excavated, the archaeologists estimated there could be as many as two to three hundred individuals buried there. It appears that only adults were buried in the mound, some of whom were buried with personal items. Children and adolescents were buried throughout the village with no burial items.[341] After burials were discovered, the new owner of the property decided to keep the site intact.

Chapter 5

WHO WERE THE FORT ANCIENT PEOPLE?

While much is known about the lifeways of the Fort Ancient people of the Ohio Valley, their ethnic identities in relation to known historic Indian tribes have eluded archaeologists and historians since their villages were first discovered. Some Ohio Valley archaeologists see the Central Algonquian–speaking Shawnee, who were in the Ohio Valley in the 1700s, as the most likely ethnic affiliation.[342] However, so far, there is no concrete evidence for a Fort Ancient–Shawnee connection or consensus among archaeologists.

The answer may be more complex. Some archeologists now think that the Fort Ancient culture may have included more than one ethnic or linguistic group. From linguistic evidence and oral traditions of the native people themselves, we know that Siouan-speaking people once occupied the Ohio Valley.[343] Sometime in the past, the Chiwere (the Iowa, Oto and Missouri) and Dhegiha Sioux (Kansa, Osage, Omaha, Quapaw and Ponca) migrated westward to their historic homelands. The Eastern Sioux, the Tutelo, Saponi, Occaneechi and Monetons migrated east probably through what is now West Virginia.

Evidence in the form of Siouan-style pottery found at certain Fort Ancient sites in West Virginia suggests that at least some of the village occupants were Siouan. Very little Siouan-style pottery has been found in Ohio or Kentucky.[344] However, other archaeological evidence from Fort Ancient villages in West Virginia, such as rectangular house patterns and Madisonville pottery, indicates a distinct connection with Ohio Valley Fort

Ancient peoples as well. The material culture (artifacts) found at these sites is also similar to that at other Fort Ancient sites.

It appears that West Virginia was an interface between Fort Ancient people to the west and Siouan-speaking people to the east. In areas where different ethnic or linguistic groups meet, there is a great deal of interaction between them. This can take the form of trade, sharing of ideas and materials and intermarriage. Since women traditionally created the pottery, there may have been a good bit of intermarriage, with Fort Ancient men taking Siouan wives. This would account for some of the Siouan-style pottery found at Fort Ancient villages in West Virginia.

So while Fort Ancient has been called a culture, it is more likely a regional cultural tradition that includes more than one ethnic or linguistic group of people. Perhaps future archaeological research will shed more light on the ethnic identities of these poorly understood people archaeologists call Fort Ancient.

GLOSSARY OF ARCHAEOLOGICAL TERMS

appendage: an addition to a main body, such as a pottery vessel. Strap handles and lugs are appendages.

applied rim strip: a strip of clay sometimes found on prehistoric pottery applied around the neck of the vessel.

artifact: an object made or used by a group of people.

ascribed status: ascribed status, as opposed to achieved status (which is earned), is a social rank that is assigned at birth or later in life.

assemblage: a group of artifacts found together that are thought to have been used at the same time by the same group of people.

beamer: a bone tool thought to be used for scraping animal hides.

biface: a stone tool or projectile point that has been worked on both sides.

calcined bone: bone that has been burned and is white in color.

castellations: a series of vertical appendages around the top of a pottery rim.

celt: a long, ground or flaked stone tool similar to an axe or adze, probably attached to a wooden handle.

chronology: a series of events arranged in the order in which they occurred.

columnella: the central whorl of a marine whelk, or similar organism, shell.

component: an occupation by a specific culture or at a specific time.

conchoidal fracture: breaking in a curved, semicircular pattern similar to ripples in a mussel shell. This usually occurs in fine-grained minerals, such as obsidian, chert (flint) and sometimes quartz.

culture: a collection of customs, language, beliefs and materials shared by a specific society; a specific group of people with shared customs, language and beliefs.

debitage: waste material left behind from the manufacture of stone tools.

faunal: pertaining to animals.

feature: archaeological evidence in the ground that cannot be removed; examples: post molds, fire hearths, storage pits.

floral: pertaining to plants.

guilloche: an incised design with a pattern of intertwining curved or angular lines found around the rims of some Ohio Valley Fort Ancient pottery vessels.

lithics: items and tools made from stone.

mammiform: shaped like a breast.

material culture: artifacts left by a specific group of people.

midden: an area in a village where trash is deposited. In late Fort Ancient villages, the midden was around the inside of the palisade wall.

multicomponent: a site that has more than one occupation over time.

ovoid: shaped like an egg.

paleoethnobotany: the analysis of prehistoric plant remains at an archaeological site.

phases of excavation: guidelines developed under Section 106 of the National Historic Preservation Act of 1966, these phases apply to all archaeological projects in the United States with federal involvement or funding: 1) Phase I (identification): to determine if an archaeological site is present; 2) Phase II (evaluation): to determine the importance of the site and determine if more work or total excavation is warranted; and 3) Phase III (mitigation/data recovery): total excavation of the site, analysis of artifacts recovered and production of technical report.

plow zone: the top layer of soil from the surface to the depth a plow might penetrate archaeological deposits.

post mold or post hole: a dark circular stain in the ground left behind after a wooden post, usually from a house or palisade wall, has decayed.

provenience: the exact location of a specific item/artifact found on a site.

punctates: decorations, usually on pottery, that are circular indentations formed with a round stick or tube pressed into clay before the vessel is fired.

saltpan: a shallow pottery vessel used for gathering salt from evaporated salt brine.

sherd: a piece of broken pottery.

stratigraphy: the layers of deposits at an archaeological site.

surface treatment: a way of roughing up the surface of a pottery vessel before firing to keep it from slipping when wet. Prehistoric potters used a variety of surface treatments, such as a cordwrapped paddle, a knotted net and even dried corncobs, on the outer surface of the vessel.

temper: material added to pottery before firing to keep it from shrinking and cracking when fired. Prehistoric potters commonly used grit (crushed rock) and crushed mussel shell for tempers.

uniface: a stone tool that is worked on only one side.

vasiform: resembling a vessel or vase.

NOTES

CHAPTER 1

1. Lepper, "Ohio Archaeology," 54.
2. Goebel, Waters and O'Rourke, "Late Pleistocene Dispersal," 1,501.
3. Sassaman, *Early Pottery in the Southeast*, 16.

CHAPTER 2

4. Pullins, Anslinger, Bradbury, Bybee, Church, Spencer and Updike, *Late Prehistoric, Late Woodland, and Late Archaic/Early Woodland Transitional Occupations*, 81.
5. Thomas, *Report on the Mound Explorations*.
6. Griffin, *Fort Ancient Aspect*.
7. Ibid.
8. Sassaman, *Early Pottery in the Southeast*, 16.
9. Hoffman, "From the Southeast," 1.
10. Brain and Phillips, *Shell Gorgets*, 401.
11. Smith and Smith, "Engraved Shell Masks in North America," 9.
12. Brashler and Moxley, "Late Prehistoric Engraved Shell Gorgets of West Virginia," 6.
13. Ibid., 1.
14. Kneberg, "Engraved Shell Gorgets and Their Associations," 19.
15. Brain and Phillips, *Shell Gorgets*, 72; Kneberg, "Engraved Shell Gorgets and Their Associations," 23; Smith and Smith, "Engraved Shell Masks in North America," 14.

16. Brain and Phillips, *Shell Gorgets*, 72–82; Drooker, "View from Madisonville," 297; Hoffman, "From the Southeast," 13.
17. Howard, "Persistence of Southern Cult Gorgets," 302.
18. Smith and Smith, "Engraved Shell Masks in North America," 15.
19. Hoffman, "From the Southeast," 17.
20. Drooker, "View from Madisonville," 301.
21. Ibid.
22. Hoffman, "From the Southeast," 17.
23. Brain and Phillips, *Shell Gorgets*, 124.
24. Hoffman, "From the Southeast," 18.
25. Smith, *Archaeology of Aboriginal Culture*, 25; Muller, "Southern Cult," 15; Hoffman, "From the Southeast," 35.
26. Hudson, *Southeastern Indians*, 421–22.

CHAPTER 3

27. Graybill, "Late Prehistoric Study Unit," 9.
28. Ibid., 10.
29. Ibid., 11–12.
30. Ibid., 12.
31. Ibid., 12–13.
32. Ibid., 14, 18.
33. Ibid., 14.
34. Ibid., 16–18.
35. Ibid. 19.
36. Ibid., 20.
37. Ibid.
38. Ibid., 23.
39. Ibid.
40. Ibid., 27–28.
41. Drooker, "View from Madisonville," 1; Tanner, *Atlas of Great Lakes Indian History*, 31–33.

CHAPTER 4

42. Broyles, "Late Archaic Component."
43. Hemmings, "West Virginia Radiocarbon Dates and Prehistory," 43.
44. Hanson, *Late 17th Century Indian Village Site*, 1.
45. Ibid.
46. Ibid., 14.
47. Ibid.

48. McMichael, "Excavations at the Buffalo Site," 15.
49. Hanson, *Late 17th Century Indian Village Site*, 23.
50. Ibid.
51. Ibid., 23–31.
52. Ibid., 31.
53. Ibid.
54. Ibid.
55. Ibid.
56. Ibid., 51.
57. Guilday, *Biological and Archeological Analysis of Bones*, 7.
58. Ibid., 10.
59. Ibid., 7.
60. Ibid.
61. Hanson, *Late 17th Century Indian Village Site*, 55–69.
62. Ibid., 56–63.
63. Ibid., 68.
64. Brain and Phillips, *Shell Gorgets*, 73; Hoffman, "From the Southeast," 20.
65. Hoffman, "From the Southeast," 20.
66. Ibid.
67. Ibid., 22.
68. Ibid.
69. Ibid.
70. Hanson, *Late 17th Century Indian Village Site*, 69, 78.
71. Ibid., 78.
72. Ibid.
73. Ibid.
74. Ibid.
75. Ibid.
76. Ibid.
77. Ibid., 79.
78. Ibid., 79–87.
79. Ibid., 79, 86.
80. Ibid., 87.
81. Ibid., 87, 89.
82. Ibid.
83. Ibid.
84. Ibid., 89–90.
85. Ibid., 91; Graybill, "Eastern Periphery of Fort Ancient (A.D. 1050–1650)," 201.
86. Hanson, *Late 17th Century Indian Village Site*, 91.
87. Evans, "Ceramic Study of Virginia Archeology," 58.
88. Spencer, "Siouan-Style Attributes on Pottery," 33.

89. Ibid.
90. Pullins, Anslinger, Bradbury, Bybee, Church, Spencer and Updike, *Late Prehistoric, Late Woodland, and Late Archaic/Early Woodland Transitional Occupations*, 5.
91. Ibid., 1.
92. Ibid.
93. Ibid.
94. Ibid., 132.
95. Ibid., 1.
96. Ibid., 234.
97. Ibid.
98. Personal communication, C. Michael Anslinger, 2016.
99. Pullins, Anslinger, Bradbury, Bybee, Church, Spencer and Updike, *Late Prehistoric, Late Woodland, and Late Archaic/Early Woodland Transitional Occupations*, 246.
100. Ibid., 401.
101. Ibid., 629.
102. Ibid., 562.
103. Ibid., 643.
104. Ibid., 703.
105. Ibid., 642.
106. Ibid., 654.
107. Church, "Appendix H."
108. Ibid.
109. Ericksen, "Appendix L."
110. Ibid.
111. Pullins, Anslinger, Bradbury, Bybee, Church, Spencer and Updike, *Late Prehistoric, Late Woodland, and Late Archaic/Early Woodland Transitional Occupations*, 564.
112. Spencer, "Siouan-Style Attributes on Pottery," 20.
113. Pullins, Anslinger, Bradbury, Bybee, Church, Spencer and Updike, *Late Prehistoric, Late Woodland, and Late Archaic/Early Woodland Transitional Occupations*, i.
114. Ibid.
115. Maslowski, Clover Archeological Site, 4.
116. Maslowski, Niquette and Wingfield, "Kentucky, Ohio and West Virginia Radiocarbon Database," 50; Freidin, "Report on the Investigations at Clover," 12.
117. Thomas, *Report on the Mound Explorations*.
118. Griffin, *Fort Ancient Aspect*, 244.
119. Ibid.
120. Ibid.

121. Ibid.
122. Adams, "Fluted Point from Cabell County," 24–25.
123. Marshall University Field School, *Clover: The Second Season.*
124. Spencer, "From the Southeast," 24.
125. Freidin, "Report on the Investigations at Clover (46CB40), West Virginia, by the Marshall University Archaeological Field School."
126. Maslowski, "Clover Site (6CB40): Nomination for National Historic Landmark Program."
127. Freidin, "Report on the Investigations at Clover," 9.
128. Ibid.
129. Marshall University Field School, *Clover: The Second Season*, 8.
130. Freidin, "Report on the Investigations at Clover," 10; Marshall University Field School, *Clover: The Second Season.*
131. Freidin, "Report on the Investigations at Clover," 10–11.
132. Ibid., 11.
133. Spencer, "Siouan-Style Attributes on Pottery," 47.
134. Marshall University Field School, *Clover: The Second Season.*
135. Ibid.
136. Ibid.
137. Ibid.
138. Ibid.
139. Cole, Bissett, Dale, Garrow, Sichler, Setzer and Marcel, *Draft Report of Archaeological Data Recovery Investigation*, 1.
140. Ibid., 5.
141. Adovasio, Dwyer, Siemon and Carlisle, *Phase I Cultural Resource Management Report.*
142. Tolonen and Bailey, *Management Summary Report.*
143. Anslinger, *Phase I Archaeological Survey.*
144. Cole, Bissett, Dale, Garrow, Sichler, Setzer and Marcel, *Draft Report of Archaeological Data Recovery Investigation*, 8.
145. Ibid.
146. Ibid.
147. Ibid., 9.
148. Ibid., 356.
149. Ibid.
150. Ibid.
151. Ibid., 380.
152. Ibid., 383.
153. Ibid., 384.
154. Ibid.
155. Ibid., 385.
156. Squier and Davis, *Ancient Monuments of the Mississippi Valley*, 293.

157. "Logan, WV History and Nostalgia."

158. McMichael, "Logan 46-Lo-4."

159. Olafson, "Logan 46-Lo-4 Revised."

160. Ibid.

161. Frye, *Technical Report*, i.

162. Ibid.

163. Ibid.

164. Ibid.

165. Ibid, 63.

166. Ibid.

167. Ibid, 32.

168. Ibid, 63.

169. Ibid.

170. Ibid.

171. Ibid.

172. Ibid, i.

173. Ibid, 89.

174. Ibid, 92.

175. Ibid, 9.

176. Ibid, 94.

177. Maslowski, "Protohistoric Villages in Southern West Virginia"; Maslowski, Niquette and Wingfield, "Kentucky, Ohio and West Virginia Radiocarbon Database," 61.

178. Pullins, Anslinger, Bradbury, Bybee, Church, Spencer and Updike, *Late Prehistoric, Late Woodland, and Late Archaic/Early Woodland Transitional Occupations*, 95.

179. Youse, "Man Site, 46Lo5," 15.

180. Ibid, 17.

181. Ibid.

182. Moxley and Bloemker, "Man Site," 3.

183. Ibid., 5.

184. Moxley, "Recent Excavations at the Man Site (46LG5)," 44.

185. Moxley and Bloemker, "Man Site," 8.

186. Ibid., 15.

187. Ibid., 17.

188. Ibid., 15.

189. Moxley, "Recent Excavations at the Man Site (46LG5)," 44; Moxley and Bloemker, "Man Site," 15.

190. Moxley and Bloemker, "Man Site," 44.

191. Moxley, "Recent Excavations at the Man Site (46LG5)," 44; Moxley and Bloemker, "Man Site," 21.

192. Spencer, "Siouan-Style Attributes on Pottery," 48.

193. Youse, "Marmet Bluffs," 42.

194. Ibid.

195. Ibid.

196. Ibid.

197. Ibid.

198. Ibid.

199. Ibid, 44.

200. Ibid.

201. Thomas, *Report on the Mound Explorations*, 411.

202. Ibid.

203. Barnett and Paxton, "Notes on Glass and Shell Beads," 31.

204. Youse, "Marmet Village," 48.

205. Ibid.

206. Spencer, "Siouan-Style Attributes on Pottery," 38.

207. Youse, "Marmet Village," 49.

208. Ibid.

209. Hoffman, "From the Southeast," 25.

210. Youse, "Marmet Village," 49.

211. Wilkins, "Miller Site (46-Ja-55)," 2.

212. Ibid.

213. Ibid., 5.

214. Ibid.

215. Ibid., 5–7.

216. Ibid., 17.

217. Ibid., 7.

218. Ibid.

219. Ibid., 13.

220. Ibid., 14–16.

221. Murphy, "Faunal Remains from the Miller Site (46-Ja-55)," 21–24, 28.

222. Ibid., 28.

223. Wilkins, "Miller Site (46-Ja-55)," 17.

224. Ibid.

225. McMichael, "Preliminary Report on Mount Carbon Village Excavations," 37.

226. Ibid.

227. Ibid.

228. Ibid., 38.

229. Ibid.

230. Ibid., 36.

231. Ibid., 43.

232. Broyles, *Fort Ancient Mortuary Customs in West Virginia*, 8.

233. Ibid., 14.

234. McMichael, "Preliminary Report on Mount Carbon Village Excavations," 42.

235. Ibid., 44.

236. Ibid., 48.

237. Ibid.

238. Guilday and Tanner, "Vertebrate Remains from the Mount Carbon Site (46-Fa-7), Fayette County, West Virginia," 1.

239. McMichael, "Preliminary Report on Mount Carbon Village Excavations, 46-Fa-7," 47.

240. Guilday and Tanner, "Vertebrate Remains from the Mount Carbon Site," 1.

241. Ibid.

242. Drooker, "View from Madisonville," 101; Hemmings, *Neale's Landing*, ch. 2, p. 18.

243. Hemmings, *Neale's Landing*, ch. 2, p. 18.

244. Ibid., ch. 3, p. 1; Hildreth, "Notes on Ohio," 161.

245. Hemmings, *Neale's Landing*, ch. 3, p. 1.

246. Ibid., pp. 1–2.

247. MacLean, "Remains on Blennerhassett Island, Ohio River," 767–64.

248. Hemmings, *Neale's Landing*, ch. 3, p. 2.

249. Baker, "Iron Axe from the Neale's Landing Site," 50–53.

250. Hemmings, *Neale's Landing*, ch. 3, p. 1.

251. Ibid., ch. 3, pp. 8–9.

252. Ibid., ch. 3, p. 11.

253. Ibid., ch. 4, p. 1.

254. Ibid., ch. 4, p. 21.

255. Ibid., ch. 5, p. 1.

256. Ibid., ch. 4, p. 22.

257. Ibid., ch. 4, p. 18.

258. Ibid., ch. 5, p. 2.

259. Ibid.

260. Ibid.

261. Ibid., ch. 5, p. 7.

262. Ibid., ch. 7, pp. 1–5.

263. Ibid., ch. 7, pp. 1–15.

264. Ibid., ch. 8, pp. 1–6.

265. Ibid., ch. 9, pp. 1–3.

266. Baker, "Iron Axe from the Neale's Landing Site," 50.

267. Pullins, Anslinger, Bradbury, Bybee, Church, Spencer and Updike, *Late Prehistoric, Late Woodland, and Late Archaic/Early Woodland Transitional Occupations*, 99.

268. Baker, "Neale's Landing Site Ceramics," 44.

269. Ibid., 45.

270. Ibid.
271. Ibid., 46–47.
272. Ibid., 48.
273. Ibid., 46
274. Ibid., 47.
275. Ibid.
276. Sassaman, *Early Pottery in the Southeast*, 41.
277. Hemmings, *Neale's Landing*, ch. 3, p. 12.
278. Ibid.
279. Moxley, "Orchard Site," 32.
280. Graybill, "Late Prehistoric Study Unit," 33.
281. Broyles, *Fort Ancient Mortuary Customs in West Virginia*, 57.
282. Moxley, "Orchard Site," 32.
283. Ibid., 34.
284. Ibid.
285. Drooker, "View from Madisonville," 317.
286. Ibid., 85.
287. Graybill, "Eastern Periphery of Fort Ancient (A.D. 1050–1650)," 222.
288. Broyles, *Fort Ancient Mortuary Customs in West Virginia*, 60.
289. Hoffman, "From the Southeast," 28.
290. Drooker, "View from Madisonville," 315.
291. Moxley, "Orchard Site," 39.
292. Bowen, "Ohio AD 400–1200."
293. Drooker, "View from Madisonville," 315.
294. Moxley, "Orchard Site," 38.
295. Ibid., 41.
296. Webb and Baby, *Adena People No. 2*, 61–71.
297. Skinner, *Social Life and Ceremonial Bundles of the Menomini Indians*, 199.
298. Drooker, "View from Madisonville," 229.
299. Burks, *Geophysical Survey at the Orchard Site*.
300. Ellis, "Investigating the Orchard Site," 42.
301. Drooker, "View from Madisonville," 83.
302. Ibid., 216.
303. Ibid., 103.
304. Thomas, *Report on the Mound Explorations*, 410.
305. Ibid.
306. Ibid.
307. Ibid.
308. Ibid.
309. Youse, "Excavation at Rolf Lee Farm Site 46-Ms-51," 15.
310. Graybill, "The Eastern Periphery of Fort Ancient (A.D. 1050-1650): A Diachronic Approach to Settlement Variability," 103.

311. Youse, "Excavation at Rolf Lee Farm Site 46-Ms-51," 15.

312. Ibid.

313. Ibid., 16.

314. Pullins, Anslinger, Bradbury, Bybee, Church, Spencer and Updike, *Late Prehistoric, Late Woodland, and Late Archaic/Early Woodland Transitional Occupations*, 100.

315. Youse, "Excavation at Rolf Lee Farm Site 46-Ms-51," 22.

316. Ibid.

317. Broyles, *Fort Ancient Mortuary Customs in West Virginia*, 37; Youse, "Excavation at Rolf Lee Farm Site 46-Ms-51," 17.

318. Youse, "Excavation at Rolf Lee Farm Site 46-Ms-51," 17.

319. Spencer, "Siouan-Style Attributes on Pottery," 42.

320. Youse, "Excavation at Rolf Lee Farm Site 46-Ms-51," 17–20.

321. Ibid., 17.

322. Ibid.

323. Ibid., 22.

324. Hoffman, "From the Southeast," 30.

325. Broyles, *Fort Ancient Mortuary Customs in West Virginia*, 37.

326. Ibid.

327. Baker, "Early Seventeenth Century Trade Beads," 23.

328. Maslowski, Niquette and Wingfield, "Kentucky, Ohio and West Virginia Radiocarbon Database," 60.

329. Graybill, "Recent Excavations in Mason County," 1–2, 10.

330. Ibid., 7.

331. Ibid.

332. Ibid., 8.

333. Ibid., 8–10.

334. Ibid., 10.

335. Graybill, "Eastern Periphery of Fort Ancient (A.D. 1050–1650)," 148.

336. Ibid., "Recent Excavations in Mason County," 12.

337. Ibid., "Eastern Periphery of Fort Ancient (A.D. 1050–1650)," 146.

338. Ibid., "Recent Excavations in Mason County," 12.

339. Ibid., 12.

340. Ibid., "Carbonized Corn from the Roseberry Farm Site," 51.

341. Ibid., "Recent Excavations in Mason County," 17.

CHAPTER 5

342. Drooker, "View from Madisonville," 103.

343. Rankin, Siouan Tribal Contacts and Dispersions, 142.

344. Personal communication David Pollack, James Morton.

BIBLIOGRAPHY

Adams, John J. "A Fluted Point from Cabell County." *West Virginia Archeologist* 12 (1960): 24–25.

Adovasio, J.M., H.P. Dwyer, E.J. Siemon III and R.C. Carlisle. *Phase I Cultural Resource Management Report for the Chelyan Bridge Replacement Project, Kanawha County, West Virginia.* Pittsburgh, PA: Department of Anthropology, University of Pittsburgh, 1986.

Anslinger, C. Michael. *Phase I Archaeological Survey of a Storm Drain Construction Corridor at the Proposed Riverside High School Site Near Diamond, Kanawha County, West Virginia.* Report Prepared by Cultural Resource Analysts, Hurricane, West Virginia. Submitted to Kanawha County Schools, Charleston, West Virginia, 1996.

Baker, Stanley W. "Early Seventeenth Century Trade Beads from the Upper Ohio Valley." *Ohio Archaeologist* 36, no. 4 (1986): 21–24.

———. "An Iron Axe from the Neale's Landing Site, 46WD39, on Blennerhassett Island." *West Virginia Archeologist* 36, no. 2 (1984): 50–53.

———. "Neale's Landing Site Ceramics: A Perspective on the Protohistoric Period from Blennerhassett Island." *West Virginia Archeologist* 40, no. (1988): 40–53.

Barnett, Roland E., and C.L. Paxton. "Notes on Glass and Shell Beads from 46-KA-9 (Marmet)." *West Virginia Archeologist* 7 (1955): 31–33.

Bowen, Jonathan E. "Ohio AD 400–1200: Village Life, the Bow and Arrow, and Corn Horticulture." Paper presented at the Society for American Archaeology, New Orleans, LA, 2001.

Brain, Jeffrey P., and Philip Phillips. *Shell Gorgets: Styles of the Late Prehistoric and Protohistoric Southeast.* Cambridge, MA: Peabody Museum of Archaeology and Ethnology, Harvard University, 1996.

Brashler, Janet G., and Ron W. Moxley. "Late Prehistoric Engraved Shell Gorgets of West Virginia." *West Virginia Archeologist* 42, no. 1 (1990): 1–10.

Broyles, Bettye J. *Fort Ancient Mortuary Customs in West Virginia.* Report of Archeological Investigations No. 7, West Virginia Geological and Economic Survey, Morgantown, WV, 1973.

———. *A Late Archaic Component at the Buffalo Site, Putnam County, West Virginia.* Report of Archeological Investigations No. 6, West Virginia Geological and Economic Survey, Morgantown, WV, 1976.

Broyles, Bettye J., Kenneth C. Reid and Darrell Fulmer. *Blennerhassett Island Archeological Project, Season 1.* West Virginia Geological and Economic Survey, Morgantown, WV, 1973.

Burks, Jarrod. *Geophysical Survey at the Orchard Site (46Ms61), a Late Prehistoric/Protohistoric Native American Site Near Point Pleasant, West Virginia. Contract Report #2009-62.* Ohio Valley Archaeology Inc., Columbus, OH, 2010.

Church, Flora. "Appendix H: Investigation of the Vertebrate Faunal Remains from the Burning Spring Branch Site (46KA142)." In *Late Prehistoric, Late Woodland, and Late Archaic/Early Woodland Transitional Occupations at the Burning Spring Branch Site on the Kanawha River, West Virginia.* By Pullins, Stevan C., C. Michael Anslinger, Andrew Bradbury, Alexandra Bybee, Flora Church, Darla Spencer and William D. Updike. Cultural Resource Analysts Inc., Contract Publication Series WV08-22. Prepared for the U.S. Army Corps of Engineers, Huntington District, Huntington, WV, 2008.

Clark, Jerry E. *The Shawnee.* Lexington: University Press of Kentucky, 1993.

Cole, Stephen C., Thaddeus G. Bissett, Emily K. Dale, Patrick H. Garrow, Judith A. Sichler, Teddi J. Setzer and Daniel L. Marcel. *Draft Report of Archaeological Data Recovery Investigation: The Dickinson Farm Site (46Ka111).* Prepared by MACTEC Engineering and Consulting Inc. Prepared for Walmart Stores Inc., 2009.

Drooker, Penelope B. "The View From Madisonville: Protohistoric Western Fort Ancient Interaction Patterns." *Memoirs of the Museum of Anthropology,* no. 31 (1997).

Ellis, Laura. "Investigating the Orchard Site (46MS61): A Protohistoric Fort Ancient Site in West Virginia." Master's thesis, Indiana University of Pennsylvania, Indiana, PA, 2015.

Ericksen, Annette G. "Appendix L." In *Late Prehistoric, Late Woodland, and Late Archaic/Early Woodland Transitional Occupations at the Burning Spring Branch Site on the Kanawha River, West Virginia.* By Pullins, Stevan C., C. Michael Anslinger, Andrew Bradbury, Alexandra Bybee, Flora Church, Darla Spencer and William D. Updike. Cultural Resource Analysts Inc.

Contract Publication Series WV08-22. Prepared for the U.S. Army Corps of Engineers, Huntington District, Huntington, WV, 2008.

———. Cultural Resource Analysts Inc. Contract Report Series WV08-22. Prepared for the U.S. Army Corps of Engineers, Huntington District, n.d.

Essenpreis, Patricia S. "Fort Ancient Settlement: Differential Response at a Mississippian–Late Woodland Interface." In *Mississippian Settlement Patterns*. Edited by B.D. Smith. New York: Academic Press, 1978: 141–67.

Evans, Clifford. "A Ceramic Study of Virginia Archeology." Smithsonian Institution Bureau of American Ethnology Bulletin 160. Washington, D.C.: United States Government Printing Office, 1955.

Freidin, Nicholas. "Report on the Investigations at Clover (46CB40), West Virginia, by the Marshall University Archaeological Field School." Manuscript on file at the State Historic Preservation Office, Charleston, WV, 1987.

Frye, Lori A., with contributions by Barbara A. Mumford, Lisa M. Dugas and Marie-Lorraine Pipes. *Technical Report: Archaeological Investigations at Site 46LG4, New State Office Building, Logan, Logan County, West Virginia*. FR No. 11-359-LG. GAI Consultants Inc. GAI Project No. C110291. Prepared for West Virginia General Services Division, 2012.

Goebel, Ted, Michael R. Waters and Dennis H. O'Rourke. "The Late Pleistocene Dispersal of Modern Humans in the Americas." *Science* 319, no. 5896 (2008): 1,497–502.

Graybill, Jeffrey Robert. "Carbonized Corn from the Roseberry Farm Site." *West Virginia Archeologist* 28 (1979): 51–53.

———. "The Eastern Periphery of Fort Ancient." *Pennsylvania Archaeologist* 54, nos. 1–2 (1984): 40–50.

———. "The Eastern Periphery of Fort Ancient (A.D. 1050–1650): A Diachronic Approach to Settlement Variability." PhD diss., University of Washington, 1981.

———. "Late Prehistoric Study Unit. Rough Draft." Manuscript on file at West Virginia Division of Culture and History, Historic Preservation Unit, Charleston, WV, 1988.

———. "Pithouses: From Indian Architecture to Suburbia." *Mountain State Geology*. West Virginia Geological and Economic Survey, December 1981.

———. "Recent Excavations in Mason County." *West Virginia Archeologist* 28 (1979): 1–23.

Griffin, James Bennett. *The Fort Ancient Aspect: Its Cultural and Chronological Position in Mississippi Valley Archaeology*. Anthropological Papers No. 26, Museum of Anthropology, University of Michigan, Ann Arbor, 1943.

Guilday, John E. *Biological and Archeological Analysis of Bones from a 17th Century Indian Village (46 PU 31), Putnam County, West Virginia*. Report of Archeological Investigation No. 4. West Virginia Geological and Economic Survey, Morgantown, WV, 1971.

Guilday, John E., and Donald P. Tanner. "Vertebrate Remains from the Mount Carbon Site (46-Fa-7), Fayette County, West Virginia." *West Virginia Archeologist* 18 (1965): 1–14.

Hanson, Lee H. *A Late 17th Century Indian Village Site (46Pu31) in Putnam County, West Virginia.* Report of Archeological Investigations No. 5. West Virginia Geological and Economic Survey. Morgantown, WV, 1975.

Hemmings, E. Thomas. *Neale's Landing: An Archeological Study of a Fort Ancient Settlement on Blennerhassett Island, West Virginia.* West Virginia Geological and Economic Survey Open File Report OF807. West Virginia Economic and Geological Survey, Morgantown, WV, 1977.

———. "West Virginia Radiocarbon Dates and Prehistory." *West Virginia Archeologist* 37, no. 2 (1985): 35–44.

Henderson, A. Gwynn, ed. *Fort Ancient Cultural Dynamics in the Middle Ohio Valley.* Monographs in World Archaeology No. 8. Madison, WI: Prehistory Press, 1992.

Hildreth, Samuel P. "Notes on Ohio." *American Journal of Science and Arts* 10 (1826): 161.

Hoffman, Darla S. "From the Southeast to Fort Ancient: A Survey of Shell Gorgets in West Virginia." *West Virginia Archeologist* 49, nos. 1–2 (1997): 1–40.

Howard, James H. "The Persistence of Southern Cult Gorgets Among the Historic Kansa." *American Antiquity* 21, no. 3 (1956): 301–3.

———. *Shawnee.* Athens: Ohio University Press, 1981.

———. "The Southern Cult in the Northern Plains." *American Antiquity*, no. 2 (1953): 130–38.

Hudson, Charles. *The Southeastern Indians.* Knoxville: University of Tennessee Press, 1976.

Kellar, James H. "Excavations at Mount Carbon." *West Virginia Archeologist* 13 (1961): 14–18.

Kneberg, Madeline. "Engraved Shell Gorgets and Their Associations." *Tennessee Archaeologist* 15, no. 1 (1959): 1–39.

Lepper, Bradley T. *Ohio Archaeology: An Illustrated Chronicle of Ohio's Ancient American Indian Cultures.* Wilmington, OH: Orange Frazier Press, 2005.

"Logan, WV History and Nostalgia." http://loganwv.us.

MacLean, J.P. "Remains on Blennerhassett Island, Ohio River." *Annual Report of the Smithsonian Institution for the Year 1882.* Washington, D.C.: Government Printing Office, 1884.

Marshall University Field School. *Clover: The Second Season.* Birke Art Gallery, MU Department of Sociology and Anthropology, Huntington, WV, 1985.

Maslowski, Robert F. Clover Archeological Site: National Register of Historic Places Registration Form. U.S. Department of the Interior, National Park Service, 1991.

———. The Clover Site (6CB40): Nomination for National Historic Landmark Program. U.S. Department of the Interior, National Park Service, 1991.

———. "Protohistoric Villages in Southern West Virginia." In *Upland Archeology in the East: Symposium 2*. Edited by Michael Barber. Atlanta, GA: USDA Forest Service Southern Region, 1984, 148–65.

Maslowski, Robert F., Charles M. Niquette and Derek M. Wingfield. "The Kentucky, Ohio and West Virginia Radiocarbon Database." *West Virginia Archeologist* 47, nos. 1–2 (1995).

McMichael, Edward V. "Excavations at the Buffalo Site, 46-Pu-31." *West Virginia Archeologist* 16 (1963): 13–23.

———. "Logan 46-Lo-4." West Virginia Archeological Site Form, Site Survey Record, 1962.

———. "Preliminary Report on Mount Carbon Village Excavations, 46-Fa-7." *West Virginia Archeologist* 14 (1962): 36–51.

———. "Summary: The Mount Carbon Stone Walls So Far." *West Virginia Archeologist* 13 (1961): 33–43.

Metress, James. "An Osteobiology of the Buffalo Site, Fulton (Putnam) County, West Virginia." Unpublished PhD diss., Department of Anthropology, Indiana University, Bloomington, September 1971.

Moxley, Ronald W. "The Orchard Site: A Proto-Historic Fort Ancient Village Site in Mason County, West Virginia." *West Virginia Archeologist* 40, no.1 (1988): 32–41.

———. "Recent Excavations at the Man Site (46LG5)." *West Virginia Archeologist* 37, no. 1 (1985): 44–46.

Moxley, Ronald W., and James D. Bloemker. "The Man Site: A Preliminary Report on a Late Prehistoric Village Site in Logan County, West Virginia." *West Virginia Archeologist* 37, no. 1 (1985): 3–22.

Muller, Jon D. "The Southern Cult." In *Southeastern Ceremonial Complex: Artifacts and Analysis*. Edited by Patricia Galloway. Lincoln: University of Nebraska, 1989, 11–26.

Murphy, James L. "Faunal Remains from the Miller Site (46-Ja-55), Jackson County, West Virginia." *West Virginia Archeologist*, no. 31 (Spring 1981): 20–30.

Olafson, Sigfus. "Logan 46-Lo-4 Revised." West Virginia Archeological Site Form, Site Survey Record, 1971.

Pullins, Stevan C., C. Michael Anslinger, Andrew Bradbury, Alexandra Bybee, Flora Church, Darla Spencer and William D. Updike. *Late Prehistoric, Late Woodland, and Late Archaic/Early Woodland Transitional Occupations at the Burning Spring Branch Site on the Kanawha River, West Virginia*. Cultural Resource Analysts Inc. Contract Publication Series WV08-22. Prepared for the U.S. Army Corps of Engineers, Huntington District, Huntington, WV, 2008.

Rankin, Robert L. Siouan Tribal Contacts and Dispersions Evidenced in the Terminology for Maize and Other Cultigens. In *Histories of Maize: Multidisciplinary Approaches to the Prehistory, Linguistics, Biogeography, Domestication, and Evolution of Maize*. Edited by John E. Staller, Robert H. Tykot and Bruce F. Benz. Boston: Academic Press, 2006, 563–75.

———. "Where Did All Those Indians Come From?" Siouan Tribes of the Ohio Valley. http://hdf.handlenet/1811/28545.

Sassaman, Kenneth E. *Early Pottery in the Southeast: Tradition and Innovation in Cooking Technology*. Tuscaloosa: University of Alabama Press, 1993.

Skinner, Alanson. *Social Life and Ceremonial Bundles of the Menomini Indians.* Anthropological Papers of the American Museum of Natural History. New York: Order of Trustees, 1913.

Smith, Marvin T. *Archaeology of Aboriginal Culture Change in the Interior Southeast: Depopulation During the Early Historical Period.* Gainesville: University Press of Florida, 1987.

———. "Early Historic Period Vestiges of the Southern Cult." In *Southeastern Ceremonial Complex: Artifacts and Analysis.* Edited by Patricia Galloway. Lincoln: University of Nebraska Press, 1989, 142–46.

Smith, Marvin T., and Julie B. Smith. "Engraved Shell Masks in North America." *Southeastern Archaeology* 8, no. 1 (1989): 9–18.

Spencer, Darla I. "Evidence of Siouan Occupation." *Virginia Quarterly Bulletin of the Archaeological Society of Virginia* 64, no. 3 (2010).

———. "Siouan-Style Attributes on Pottery from Late Prehistoric and Protohistoric Sites in Southern West Virginia." *West Virginia Archeologist* 58, nos. 1–2 (2006): 1–52.

Squier, E.G., and E.H. Davis. *Ancient Monuments of the Mississippi Valley: Comprising the Results of Extensive Original Surveys and Explorations.* 1847. Clarified and copyrighted 1992 by Arthur W. McGraw.

Swanton, John R. *The Indians of the Southeastern United States.* Washington, D.C.: Smithsonian Institution Press, 1946.

Tanner, Helen Hornbeck, ed. *Atlas of Great Lakes Indian History.* The Civilization of the American Indian Series. Norman: University of Oklahoma Press, 1987.

Taylor, Colin F., ed. *Native American Myths and Legends.* New York: Smithmark Publishers, 1994.

Thomas, Cyrus. *Report on the Mound Explorations of the Bureau of Ethnology.* Classics of the Smithsonian Anthropology. Washington, D.C.: Smithsonian Intuition Press, 1985.

Tolonen, Anthony, and Doug Bailey. *Management Summary Report of Phase I Archaeological Investigations at the Proposed Quincy School Project, Kanawha County, West Virginia.* Report Prepared by KEMRON Environmental Services, Cincinnati. Submitted to Kanawha County Schools, Charleston, WV, 1995.

Webb, William S., and Raymond S. Baby. *The Adena People No. 2*. Columbus: Ohio State University Press, 1957.

Wilkins, Gary R. "The Miller Site (46-Ja-55): A Fort Ancient Component." *West Virginia Archeologist*, no. 31 (1981): 2–30.

Youse, Hillis J. "Excavation at Rolf Lee Farm Site 46-Ms-51." *West Virginia Archeologist* 18 (1965): 15–24.

———. "The Man Site, 46Lo5." *West Virginia Archeologist* 25 (1976): 15–19.

———. "The Marmet Bluffs—Archeological Site 46Ka7." *West Virginia Archeologist* 38, no. 1 (1986): 42–44.

———. "Marmet Village—Archeological Site 46KA9." *West Virginia Archeologist* 40, no. 1 (1988): 47–49.

INDEX

ABOUT THE AUTHOR

Darla Spencer (Hoffman) is a registered professional archaeologist (RPA) who was born and still lives in Charleston, West Virginia. She has researched the archaeology and early history of West Virginia for over twenty years. In 2002, she was awarded the Sigfus Olafson Award of Merit for her contributions to West Virginia archaeology by the West Virginia Archeological Society (WVAS).

Currently retired, Spencer is the secretary-treasurer of the WVAS and a board of directors member of the Council for West Virginia Archaeology. She has published several articles in the *West Virginia Archeologist* and the *Virginia Quarterly Bulletin* journals and authored several entries in the *West Virginia Encyclopedia*. She also developed and currently teaches online classes on the mound building cultures and the early Native Americans in West Virginia through the Native American Studies Program at West Virginia University.